GREAT WESTERN STEAM
1934-1949

Churchward 2-8-0 No. 2808, built in 1905 as one of the earliest members of the class, wheels a lengthy westbound Class 'H' freight towards Uphill Junction. This is at the western end of the section of the original Bristol & Exeter main line which avoided passing through the station at Weston-super-Mare, Norman Lockett's home town. *Photograph taken at 11.35am on Monday, 8th March 1948*

The stirring sight of a pair of 'Castle' Class 4-6-0s, No. 5081 *Penrice Castle* and No. 5067 *St Fagans Castle*, heading their train across Blackwood Viaduct, just to the east of Cornwood station, on the climb towards the summit at Wrangaton. The train is the 1.00pm (Sundays) Newquay-Paddington, and the date is 6th August 1939, just four weeks before the commencement of the Second World War. Based on the evidence of the many hundreds of photographs featuring main line GW motive power as recorded by Norman Lockett, the use of a pair of 'Castles' was by no means a regular practice. At the time, No. 5081, which had entered service only three months previously, was allocated to Wolverhampton, Stafford Road and may have been used here as 'assisting engine' as a convenient means of getting the locomotive back from Plymouth to its next scheduled working. No. 5081 was destined to be renamed *Lockheed Hudson* in January 1941, the penultimate member of a group of a dozen 'Castles' given the names of famous aircraft following the Battle of Britain in autumn 1940.

GREAT WESTERN STEAM
1934-1949

MIKE ARLETT & DAVID LOCKETT

Lightmoor Press

Like several of his contemporaries in the 1930s, Norman Lockett only occasionally visited and photographed scenes from the branch lines, much preferring the excitement of recording motive power hard at work on the main line. So, it is always a delight for the authors to come across a branch line scene such as this in Norman's collection of glass plates, featuring 2-6-2T No. 4591 with the 5.25pm Plymouth Millbay to Tavistock train, near Clearbrook. *21st June 1938*

FRONT COVER PICTURE: 4-4-0 No. 3446 *Goldfinch* assists No. 6001 *King Edward VII* up Hemerdon Incline with the 10.30am (Sundays) Plymouth to Paddington express. *13th August 1939 (See also pages 78-9)*

REAR COVER PICTURE: Under a threatening sky, No. 4932 *Hatherton Hall* was captured with the 5.15pm stopping train from Plymouth to Truro, climbing the gradient towards Trerule Foot, on an exposed section of the Cornish main line to the west of St. Germans. *1st August 1939*

THE NORMAN LOCKETT ARCHIVE – A NOTE FROM THE PUBLISHER

Norman Lockett's archive of mainly glass plate negatives of the railways of south and west England constitute what must now be one of the last great mostly unpublished photographic collections. Although the Great Western, a railway he began taking pictures of when it was still in its prime, was his first love, he also ranged over the Somerset & Dorset (covered in our first volume), the Southern Region of British Railways and some of the industrial lines of the east Midlands and far beyond. He had an eye for a good location, many of which seem not to have been 'discovered' by other noted photographers, and a number of them feature within these pages. When he found a location he liked, he tended to return there on numerous occasions. Others, such as around Weston-super-Mare, were simply handy, being close to home for an evening's foray out photographing trains. Consequently, anyone leafing through these pages will find certain locations repeated quite frequently. However, two factors, we believe, fully justify this repetition and will serve to hold the reader's attention through to the last page. Firstly, the superb quality of the images, which again have been scanned directly from the original plates, all lovingly preserved by David Lockett. Secondly, the sheer variety of trains depicted. We live in an age where it is generally possible to predict what the next train which passes will look like. Whether freight or passenger, it will undoubtedly be uniform in its monotony – all carriages looking the same or a long rake of identical wagons hauled by one of around half a dozen different types of locomotive, whichever part of the country you may be in. The photographs within these pages will take you back to a gentler age, when the next train might be hauled by a 'King', a 'Star' a 'Bulldog' or a 'Prairie', and comprise several different types (and ages) of coaches from perhaps more than one company, or maybe twenty different types of goods wagon. Such was the joy of photographing trains or simply 'trainspotting' in the age of steam. We do not apologise, therefore, for the fact that, on occasion within, you will find yourself standing in the same place for several pages. Simply sit back and enjoy the thrill of being able to watch an unexpected variety of trains passing by, courtesy of a master of his art.

THE NORMAN LOCKETT ARCHIVE

CONTENTS

Published by LIGHTMOOR PRESS
© Lightmoor Press, Mike Arlett & David Lockett 2010
Designed by Mike Arlett & Neil Parkhouse

British Library Cataloguing-in-Publication Data. A catalogue record for this book is available from the British Library
ISBN 13: 9781899889 46 4

LIGHTMOOR PRESS
Unit 144B, Lydney Trading Estate, Harbour Road, Lydney, Gloucestershire GL15 5EJ
www.lightmoor.co.uk
Lightmoor Press is an imprint of Black Dwarf Lightmoor Publications Ltd

Printed & bound by TJ International, Padstow, Cornwall

FOREWORD

The modest success, favourable comments and reviews received following the publication of *The Somerset & Dorset Railway 1935-1966* have encouraged us to offer this, the first of two further volumes from the 'Norman Lockett Archive' which feature the Great Western Railway. As we mentioned in the introduction to our previous book, there can be no doubt that Norman was, above all, an unashamed enthusiast of steam motive power designed and built for the GWR. This volume covers the years from 1934 until 1949, although excluding the period of the Second World War, during which time Norman took no photographs. Part Two will cover the era from 1950 and a wider geographical area, when the rails of the former Great Western system were (as is sometimes still argued) somewhat sullied by the appearance of the BR 'Standard' classes of locomotive designs.

First, however, a word of caution! If you are expecting a book which illustrates locations spread far and wide across what was once the territory of the Great Western Railway, then this volume is definitely not for you. For reasons we will explain, the core geographical area featured herein extends from Weston-super-Mare to reach only as far as south-east Cornwall, along the original GW route to the West of England. There is, in addition, the occasional foray into the Bristol area and to just a few of the branch lines. Like some of his contemporaries from the 1930s, Norman appears to have found photographing main line scenes far more rewarding than a visit to a local branch line. We also wish to point out that, despite the title, a few 'interlopers' have found their way into this tome – not least because the period covered includes the 'locomotive exchanges' in 1948.

As with our 'Somerset & Dorset' book, we have attempted to ensure that this volume contains only a minority of Norman Lockett's photographs which have appeared before in any other publication. In some cases, a picture has been re-used if it happens to feature the only (or a rare) occasion when Norman photographed a specific location or viewpoint. Otherwise, our only justification for republishing a photograph is because of the great technological advances made in the past decade, enabling scans to be made directly from Norman's original glass plate negatives rather than from his own prints. This is particularly relevant to the earliest, pre-war, photographs taken in and around Plymouth, where we admit to the re-use of a slightly larger

David Lockett (left) and his older brother Geoff (right) were obviously both introduced to the Great Western lineside at an early age, as evidenced here by this delightful family photograph taken by Norman's wife, Louise, in the summer of 1938. David recounts the location as being 'near Hemerdon'.

percentage of previously published views, although, to the best of our knowledge, even these have not been reprinted for some twenty years. We are retaining the same format and style as per our first book with Lightmoor Press, including a large number of full page pictures and just a few spread across two pages. So, our apologies again for the amount of book turning that is required but – having regard to the format of Norman's original glass plate negatives – in our opinion (and that of our publisher) this really is the best way to reproduce many of these high quality photographs. Generally speaking, we have also persisted with a time-related theme, to take you through from Norman's earliest photographs until reaching the summer of 1949.

In our introduction to *The Somerset & Dorset Railway 1935-1966*, we mentioned the constraints imposed upon Norman by a 5½ day working week and a reliance on public transport. The same applies here, both factors restricting, throughout the period covered in this book, when and where he could pursue his great interest in railway photography. It is also evident that Norman generally preferred to photograph the train, whenever possible, out in the countryside, even if, during the early years, he travelled for example only as far from his home in Plymouth as the lineside at Hemerdon Incline.

We also emphasised in our earlier book, that Norman's style was heavily influenced by many of his contemporaries dating from the pre-Second World War era; the likes of Casserley, Earley, Gordon Tidy, Hamilton Ellis, Hebron, Nunn, Soole and Wethersett are just a few names which spring to mind. Norman later became a member of the Railway Photographic Society and an exponent of the 'three-quarter front view', although – as will again be evident in this book – he was far from averse to including in some his compositions, much of the background detail, even if subsequently, in making a print, he elected to omit most of the latter. This was obviously a case of 'Old habits die hard'!

Other than from the period 1934 to 1938, Norman used a large, quarter plate size, Thornton-Pickard Reflex camera exposing glass plate negatives. His earlier camera, using smaller 3½ins x 2½ins glass plates, was retained (and generally also carried by him) as a back-up for emergencies. Each camera was carried in its own case, in which were also stored a slide-holder loaded with unused and exposed glass plates. Now just compare that lot with the convenience of today's digital cameras! Most of his photography was carried out between the months of April and October. Development of the glass plate negatives would be undertaken, by Norman, late at night, usually within a week or so of the photographs having been taken. Printing, enlarging and mounting would be left until the 'closed' season – November to March. Norman's professional training as a chemist served him well in both the development and printing of his photographs. However, as with *The Somerset & Dorset Railway 1935-1966,* in order to present Norman's work at its best we have returned to the original glass plates for the scanning process, rather than merely make use of the existing prints produced, many years ago, by Norman.

The earliest of Norman's negatives are (as at 2010) more than seventy-five years old, with the later ones featured in this book now a mere sixty-one years! Despite the collection having been stored very carefully by David, in some instances the passing years have taken their toll. Indeed, there are a considerable number of interesting pictures which we have been able to include only because it is now possible to 'repair', by means of digital imaging software, much of the deterioration to the emulsion (fogging, scratches, pin holes, watermarking, etc) on the original glass plates. Even so, we apologise in advance for those (hopefully) few instances where the results of such remedial action may appear rather too obvious. As Mike has checked the scan of each glass plate, there have been times when his sanity has been severely tested. Just why did the flaws on so many negatives reveal themselves amongst a plethora of lineside overhead wires rather than in the open sky?

We must again express our profound thanks to our publishing team and, in particular, Neil Parkhouse who, we were certain, would never wish to deal with us again! The trouble that Neil and his team, and the printer, have taken is, we trust, self-evident when looking carefully at the quality of reproduction achieved. We hope you enjoy the results of our combined labours. As ever, we are grateful to our wives, Sandra and Daphne, for putting up again with our continued frequent defections from domestic labours. Our acknowledgements follow, as in time (we hope) will Part Two.

Mike Arlett & David Lockett, 2010

ACKNOWLEDGEMENTS

Looking through Norman's very large selection of photographs, it soon became apparent what a diversity of coaching stock had been in use on the GWR. Even to our untrained eyes, it sometimes seemed that just about every vehicle forming a single passenger train appeared to be different, a point Mike mentioned to our publisher. This led to the suggestion that we should try to identify and comment on interesting or unusual examples as portrayed in Norman's photographs. Well, that's fine, except for one rather large problem – this is a subject about which both David and Mike admit to having little to no knowledge! Fortunately, our publisher was able to put Mike in touch with John Lewis, the author of several books and articles on GWR coaching stock. John willingly 'took up the challenge' and has provided Mike with much detailed information, for which we wish to record our most grateful thanks. As we were to discover from John, it was not only the varied designs which are of interest but the often complex workings by which the GWR maximised the use of much of its coaching stock. We hope this information will add to your enjoyment of this book. Where, in a few cases, there was doubt, John has also been of considerable help in attempting to identify some of the train services featured herein.

Our thanks also to Chris Osment, who has clarified and confirmed various queries regarding signalling at several of the locations featured within this book. Invaluable help has been provided by Brian Macdermott, who has responded to queries from Mike necessitating access to a number of GWR Working Time Tables.

The patience and resolve of David Stubbs must be acknowledged, for it was he who gave of his time and car to transport Mike around the many narrow (some very narrow!) lanes between Wellington and Whiteball Tunnel to establish or confirm the exact whereabouts of some of the photographs appearing in this book; a pleasant but sometimes frustrating task in which we succeeded in all but a single instance. Suffice to say, the scenery at these locations is generally *very* different to when photographed by Norman all those years ago.

Special thanks are again due to Richard Strange, who, by the way, happens to be the 'S' of 'The HSBT Project' (*see page 152*). It was he who suggested Mike could be the first to take advantage of data already gathered by the Project which, when completed, will be published as a series covering, in turn, each of the old BR Regions. Richard, with his customary promptness, has responded or redirected Mike's various queries to the appropriate expert. Also thanks to Richard Ball, whose knowledge of West Coast Joint Stock helped confirm these 'alien' vehicles (well 'alien' to Mike – who hails from Wiltshire!), a few examples of which will be noted amongst the pages of this book.

We must also acknowledge two web sites to which Mike has turned for help: *The Great Western Archive* (www.greatwestern.org.uk) and an impressive site for anybody wishing to know just about anything regarding the history of Plymouth – www.plymouthdata.info

As was the case with *The Somerset & Dorset Railway 1935-1966,* we wish to acknowledge Mike's considerable use of the *Railway Observer,* the house magazine of the Railway Correspondence & Travel Society, which provides such a wonderful source of motive power and associated information. How good that the RCTS is now digitising issues of the *Railway Observer* for various years and marketing each annual set on a CD-ROM. Mike has also drawn freely (some might argue plundered!) from what has been previously published in the *Railway Magazine, Trains Illustrated* and many of the books and articles which have been written over the years about the GWR. Not least amongst these are the various titles penned by O.S. Nock, including his two-part monograph *The GWR Stars, Castles & Kings,* published by David & Charles. Much more recently (2009), Irwell Press has published *The Book of the Castle 4-6-0s* by Ian Sixsmith, which provides a detailed record of every member of this famous class of locomotive. Mike makes no claims as to originality of information other, perhaps, than in relation to some of the asides which, it is hoped, might add a little to your enjoyment of this book.

Showing a lovely clean exhaust, albeit with a load unlikely to overtax a 'King', No. 6003 *King George IV* passes the Up Distant signal for Hemerdon box, with the 11.10am Penzance-Paddington express. The locomotive will have taken over the express at Plymouth and, with the time recorded by Norman as 2.15pm, nears the top of Hemerdon Incline. This extends from a point just to the east of Plympton station (closed March 1959) as far as the approach to Hemerdon Signal Box (closed December 1973), a distance of about 2.7 miles. The long straight, seen here, leading towards the summit is graded at 1 in 42 (although at least one official reference states 1 in 41), before easing to 1 in 75. Once past this point, there are about a further 7½ miles of adverse gradients which, other than two very short respites, are continuous but involve much less severe climbing in order to reach the summit at Wrangaton, about 14¼ miles out from North Road station. *12th June 1934*

SECTION 1
THE MID-1930s

David Lockett has never established what first persuaded his father to take up railway photography. The earliest photographs in the collection date from 1st April 1934, by which time Norman had only recently married and left his home town of Weston-super-Mare (in Somerset) to work and live in Plymouth. Norman spent his entire working life in the employment of Boots the Chemist, joining the firm in 1925 to commence four years as an apprentice, followed by a similar period as a student at the Merchant Venturers' College of Pharmacy in Bristol. In early April 1933, he was registered as a chemist and druggist, becoming a member of the Pharmaceutical Society and moving to Plymouth. His training as a chemist was to serve him well when it came to developing and making his own photographic prints.

Perhaps this new interest came about because, following eight years of training and study, he needed to take up a hobby to provide some form of 'escapism', to occupy what very little spare time he could at last enjoy. Within a year of his transfer to Plymouth, Norman appears to have taken his first railway photographs, mostly at locations within a short distance from his new home. The road at the side of his house terminated at some railings which formed the boundary of the GWR, just to the east of North Road station – a very convenient place to pause for a few minutes and watch the passing traffic in and out of the station. Was this, David and I have wondered, what triggered Norman's affinity with railway photography, or had this already been fostered as a child when living in Weston? Whatever the reason, it is evident he decided, from the start, that he much preferred the countryside and not a busy railway station as the backcloth to the great majority of his photographic compositions.

Limited to the use of public transport, Norman tended to venture no further than could be comfortably reached by local train or bus to permit a few hours at a chosen location on a single weekday afternoon or a Sunday, the only times, holidays excluded, usually available during an otherwise busy working week.

It has been claimed that only the most partisan of railway historians might attempt to deny that, at the start of the 1930s, the Great Western Railway still led the field in terms of locomotive design and performance within the British Isles. By the time Norman Lockett exposed a first glass plate negative by the lineside just four years later, Swindon's dominance in design was about to be challenged.

Little more than five years since released new into traffic, No. 4911 *Bowden Hall* nears the top of Hemerdon Incline with the 12.30pm Plymouth to Newton Abbot stopping train. The coaching stock comprises three clerestory carriages designed by Dean and constructed 35-40 years earlier. The leading coach appears to be a corridor brake third, somewhat in need of a repaint; the second is possibly a non-gangway brake tri-composite (brake 1st/3rd by the date this picture was taken) with lavatories. It may have had its guard's lookouts removed. The third coach appears to be another brake third. *1st May 1934*
No. 4911 was destined to remain in traffic for only another seven years, as this was the locomotive which suffered a near-direct hit by a bomb at Keyham on 29th April 1941, during one of the many terrible air raids on Plymouth. The locomotive was so badly damaged that it was taken to Swindon, formally withdrawn on 10th June 1941, and cut up. This is the earliest of Norman's GWR photographs in the collection which David has now held for more than thirty years. David is convinced there were just a few earlier glass plates from April 1934 but, to date, their whereabouts remain a mystery.

Mid-afternoon finds No. 4901 *Adderley Hall* heading westwards from Cornwood with a Down stopping train from Newton Abbot to Plymouth. *12th June 1934*
No. 4901 was the first real 'Hall' Class 4-6-0, built at Swindon in 1928 (part of Lot No. 254). No. 4900, bearing the name Saint Martin, had been rebuilt by the GWR in 1924 as a modification of 'Saint' Class No. 2925 and so became the pioneer of these very successful mixed traffic, two-cylinder 4-6-0s, the last of which was built in 1943. However, a further seventy-one examples of a modified design were constructed between 1944 and November 1950. For such a short train, the variety of the stock is of interest, all of Victorian designs. At the rear is a relatively modern corridor third. We are advised that the leading coach is a non-gangway brake third and appears to have four compartments. It is probably Diagram D24. The second coach appears to be a composite, possibly to Diagram E47 and to a layout of which only two (No's 7590(1) were built for the South Wales Corridor trains in 1896. The third coach appears to be a low roof 40ft passenger luggage van to diagrams K14, K15 or K16, whilst bringing up the rear is a Collett 'high waist' third class corridor coach. (You can appreciate now why we needed the assistance of acknowledged expert John Lewis in such matters!)

OUT AND ABOUT IN 1934

This appears to be Norman's only visit to this location which he described as '*near Wearde*'. Perhaps he was put off by the telegraph poles positioned on the side of the line from which he photographed 'Castle' Class No. 4075 *Cardiff Castle* climbing towards St. Germans with a Wolverhampton to Penzance express. Unusually, he failed to retain a record of the exact date, noting only the time as 5.15pm and the month as September 1934. In any case, Norman had already discovered a lineside location in this area of south-east Cornwall just six miles west of here, which was obviously much more to his liking and which we first feature on page 21. In fact, we think he may have been scouting for new locations when he took the photograph above, probably deciding, there and then, this viewpoint was 'not up to scratch'. There is no evidence to suggest he ever made a print from this negative.
Not knowing this locality in any detail, David and I remain less than fully confident as to where, exactly, this scene was photographed. My money is towards the eastern end of the inland diversionary route opened by the GWR to passenger traffic between Wearde (near Saltash) and St. Germans in 1908.

Initial thoughts that this photograph might have been taken during a half-day trip to the seaside at Goodrington were soon dispelled when we discovered that Norman, rather than taking to the beach, returned inland to take some lineside shots at Totnes! Against the backdrop of Torbay, Churchward 'Mogul' No. 4344 climbs the bank from Goodrington towards Churston, with a local train to Kingswear. Norman recorded the lighting as '*brilliant*' but that didn't necessarily equate to the temperature and, judging from the apparent dearth of bathers taking to the waters, perhaps the sea had yet to warm up that summer. *10th July 1934*

'Bulldog' 4-4-0 No. 3336 *Titan* assists No. 6011 *King James 1* with the 5.30am Paddington-Penzance (mail) along the section of quadruple track from Newton Abbot on the approach to Aller Junction, where the main line to Plymouth and Cornwall swings away south-westwards from the branch to Torbay and Kingswear. The 4-4-0, probably attached to the train at Newton Abbot, had been built in 1900 (originally numbered 3348) and survived in service only another eighteen months after being photographed here. No. 6011 had clocked up a mere six years in service and was allocated to Old Oak Common. *31st July 1934*

This should prove a fascinating photograph for those interested in GWR stock workings. The train, which travelled via Bristol, carried a PO Van (or 'Letter Car' as described by the GWR) as far west cs Taunton, whilst three vehicles were collected and no less than nine vehicles (Siphon Gs and various vans) were dropped off en route. The train appears to consist of two non-corridor third class clerestory coaches, a Siphon G van, a Dean 40ft low roof passenger brake van (which had lost its lookouts and might have been in use as a stores van), a clerestory brake third (van third in GWR speak), a Collett coach and a 'Dreadnought' (of which one end is just visible). There are no doubt more vehicles forming the rear of the train, the makeup of which was, on this Tuesday, somewhat at variance with that listed in the GWR's Through Coaches Book for July 1934. It looks as if a Siphon G had been substituted for one of the scheduled brake vans and the train was being used to move that pair of non-corridor clerestory thirds down the line.

TOTNES

On his return from Goodrington to Plymouth on Tuesday, 10th July 1934, Norman stopped off at Totnes station in the early evening. Having taken just one photograph at the station, he set off to find a position by the lineside little more than a quarter mile to the west, close to where the railway commences the climb towards Rattery.

Just one digit out! At 6.05pm, the 1.30pm Down Paddington-Penzance express, hauled here by No. 5030 *Shirburn Castle***, passes the base of the hillside the top of which is dominated by Totnes Castle, just out of view in this photograph and which gave its name to No. 5031. When photographed here, No. 5030 had been in traffic just two months and was based at Exeter shed.** *10th July 1934*
As mentioned in the 'Acknowledgements' section of this book, the GWR was notorious for mixing coach styles on trains. Here we have the first four coaches of an express showing four different styles and, co-incidentally, in date order. The leading coach appears to be a wide-bodied first class sleeping car of 1930 vintage, which ran on 6-wheeled bogies. It is presumably working down empty. The second coach is a 70ft brake third of 1922-5, often referred to as 'South Wales' stock. The third coach is a 70ft 'Toplight' third of 1908-21 period and the fourth coach is a 'Concertina' of 1906-7.

OPPOSITE PAGE TOP: At the same location just twenty minutes later, No. 5026 *Criccieth Castle* **(released into traffic just a month prior to No. 5030 and based at Newton Abbot) passes by and commences to attack Rattery Incline with the 9.15am Liverpool-Plymouth express.** *10th July 1934*
After the earliest years of his photography, it becomes apparent that Norman would contemplate far less frequently photographing a passing train unless he could include all of it in his viewfinder. However, the interest here is the second vehicle, No. 1070, built as one of the brake vans for the GWR's 1896 Royal Train. By 1934, it was in use as a Hotels Department Refreshment Van. It would have been sent down from Paddington earlier in the day and attached to this train at Taunton. It was fortuitous that Norman selected a Tuesday for this lineside visit, corresponding with the only day of the week this van travelled west by this service.

OPPOSITE PAGE BOTTOM: Large 'Prairie' No. 3152 pauses between banking duties beside the Down platform at Totnes station. Carrying a No. 3 target identification board, No. 3152 was one of a stud of these Churchward 2-6-2Ts allocated to Newton Abbot. Situated at the bottom of heavy inclines in both directions, the bankers were required at Totnes to assist both east and westbound freight traffic. No. 3152 was built in 1907 and, certainly in her later years, was engaged in assisting traffic through the Severn Tunnel, before withdrawal from service in December 1946. By the way, notice the posters on the station wall commending the benefits of travelling by train and forwarding luggage in advance and also the once-familiar enamel advertisement featuring 'Stephens Ink'. Much of this side of the station was destroyed by a fire in mid April 1962.

HEMERDON

I wanted to bring you back to near the top of Hemerdon Incline before moving much farther 'down the bank', because I was intrigued by the second carriage featured in this train, which was identified for us, by Richard Ball, as an ex-West Coast Joint Stock (L&NW & Caledonian Joint) 12-wheeled, W9 composite dining car, 9ft wide with kitchen in the centre and looking very dirty. Apparently, these vehicles were regularly to be seen on workings between the West Country, the North West and Scotland in the 1930s. The motive power is provided by 'Star' Class No. 4034 *Queen Adelaide* which, just a couple of years earlier, had been fitted with outside steam pipes. Norman recorded the train as the 1pm Plymouth (Millbay) to Liverpool express. *12th June 1934 Examples of vehicles such as the ex-L&NWR carriage seen here appear in several of Norman's photographs which feature these 'port to port' and certain other services during the pre-Second World War period.*

We visited this same viewpoint on page 8 but this slightly wider angle provides a magnificent sight of No. 4079 *Pendennis Castle* about to pass the Hemerdon Up Distant signal. In the background, the double track falls at a gradient of 1 in 42, before curving out of sight through the heavily wooded section about mid-distance on the climb. Norman Lockett found another location farther down the incline, which we will visit on the next page. *12th June 1934*

Built in February 1924, at the time of Norman's photograph No. 4079 was based at Stafford Road, so this train may well have been the 10.45am Penzance to Wolverhampton. Certainly the timing recorded by Norman at Hemerdon (1.55pm) and the formation of the train add to this conclusion: a 'Toplight' brake third, a Collett 'high waist' (post-1929), flush window composite, a dining car, followed by a third and brake third. Norman referred to the train as the 'Up Cornishman', a famous name harking back to broad gauge days but re-introduced briefly for the summer of 1935 (the GWR Centenary year) for the 10.35am Paddington relief to the Down 'Cornish Riviera'. Norman may have added the information many years later, when re-cataloguing his earliest glass plates, by which time (from June 1952) BR Western Region had utilised the name for the 10.30am Penzance-Wolverhampton and 9.15am departure in the reverse direction.

LOWER HEMERDON – 1

The 'Cornish Riviera Express' is lifted up the long incline about a mile east of Plympton station by the combined efforts of 'Bulldog' Class 4-4-0 No. 3305 (formerly named *Tintagel*) and 'King' Class 4-6-0 No. 6010 *King Charles 1*. No. 3305 was a rebuild from one of the 'Duke' Class (No. 3269, dating from 1896), the name *Tintagel* being re-used until removed in 1930. The locomotive was withdrawn just two years after being seen here. *11th September 1936*

Just as an aside, I recall from my schooldays the good advice given to always look through an entire exam paper before commencing to write any answers. Well, all these years later, I have discovered that the same principle needs to be applied when researching photographs from Norman Lockett's photographic collection! On more than one occasion I have spent considerable time trying to establish exactly where Norman had been standing only to find that when he returned there, perhaps some years later, another of his photographs just happens to reveal a lineside milepost! Have a look at page 53 to see an example of what I mean. Norman often excluded such extraneous detail by not printing the full width or height of the negative, so this has proved to be just one of the advantages in scanning the photographs for this book from the original glass plates. Unfortunately, over many years, this particular glass plate negative has become badly scratched, so here is an example of where, with the aid of digital imaging software and a lot of patience, virtually all of the damage has been 'repaired' – it was just too good a picture to leave out, especially as Norman only occasionally resorted to a 'low angle' shot!

The external condition of No. 4940 *Ludford Hall* indicates the locomotive has either returned from a recent visit to Works which included a full repaint or has received the 'full treatment' by the depot cleaners. Even the exhaust is 'clean'! The paintwork positively glistens in the late-morning sunshine as she passes by with an eastbound train. Built only five years earlier, the locomotive had first been allocated to **Taunton**. *23rd October 1954*

Norman returned to this section of the incline time and time again. David forwarded me nearly fifty scans from plates featuring what was obviously one of his father's favourite locations during the pre-war years. My problem has been which few to include in this book, so I hope you will forgive me when I bring you back here briefly on at least two more occasions!

INTO CORNWALL

Other than the Torpoint and Saltash ferries, this was the only option available for crossing the River Tamar between Plymouth and Saltash until the road bridge was opened in October 1961. Taken in September 1934, this is the view of the Royal Albert Bridge from the northern end of the Up platform at Saltash station – it was one of *very* few photographs taken by Norman Lockett which did not include a train! An Up service is signalled across the single line bridge. Prominent in the right foreground, notice the 'setting down post' for the single line token which authorised passage for the 924 yards from the Royal Albert Bridge Signal Box on the Plymouth side of the river.

The first of the weekday motor services departed here for Plymouth at 6.16am. Thereafter, a frequent shuttle service by rail continued until the last train reached Saltash after 11pm and this intensity of operation remained little changed until the opening of the Tamar Road Bridge.

With the blower on, 2-8-0 No. 2839 pauses at Bodmin Road to take on water before proceeding westwards with a Class 'D' freight. It appears this was the only occasion Norman took a photograph here, the farthest west into Cornwall to which he travelled with his camera. It was possibly an afternoon trip from Plymouth by rail to 'scout' for potential lineside locations which he might visit. *15th August 1934*
This is one of the pictures which has been published before but the original glass plate had been damaged, with the extreme bottom right-hand corner missing. However, again with the aid of digital imaging software, the missing corner has been 'reinstated'.

Just into its third year of service, Truro-based 4-6-0 No. 5902 *Howick Hall* takes advantage of an easing of the grades, marking the end of the worst of the climb westwards from St. Germans. The train was the 1.30pm **Paddington-Penzance**, which No. 5902 would have taken over at Plymouth around twenty minutes earlier. Norman noted the time as 7.10pm. *18th July 1934*

This rural location was, perhaps, spotted by Norman from the train and subsequently revisited on several occasions during the following five years. Initially recorded by him as 'near St. Germans', he later used the more accurate description of 'near Trerule Foot', which helped me narrow it down somewhat! However, it was the use of the larger format glass plate negatives at this same location in 1939 (see page 86) which provided the clue to the exact whereabouts. David thinks his father probably travelled here from Plymouth via the Torpoint Ferry and then by a Torpoint to Liskeard bus.

AN INTERLUDE WEST OF TAUNTON

One of Taunton's allocation of '4575' Class 2-6-2Ts heads down the Minehead Branch on a Thursday afternoon with a local from Taunton. The bridge under which the train has just passed is 'Norton Bridge', the first on the branch after leaving the main line at Norton Fitzwarren. Note that the 2-6-2T carries a token exchanger, fitted in July 1933 but not brought into use until 6th July 1934, just two months after Norman took this photograph. *3rd May 1934*

The Norton Fitzwarren to Bishop's Lydeard section of the branch line was subsequently doubled and, as such, brought into use by July 1936; the original track seen here becoming the 'Down' line. Following closure to passenger traffic on 4th January 1971 and with goods traffic having already been withdrawn in July 1964, the branch line closed. In the late 1970s, the original (Down) line was lifted by the West Somerset Railway, who took over the branch as a heritage railway. More recently, early in 2006, they have installed a set of points here (facing towards Norton Fitzwarren and now known as 'Allerford Junction') to provide access to a new triangular layout which, when complete, will enable the WSR to turn locomotives and stock at the eastern end of this superb heritage railway.

A week later, Norman Lockett revisited the same location. However, we are now looking in a westerly direction, as an unidentified Collett '2251' Class 0-6-0 approaches the junction with the main line at Norton Fitzwarren, hauling a Minehead to Taunton branch line freight. *10th May 1934*

Having visited the Minehead Branch near Norton Fitzwarren on two successive Thursday afternoons, the following week found Norman at the side of the main line at 4pm on a rather overcast afternoon. *'Near Wellington'* was all he recorded as to the location! Newton Abbot based No. 5019 *Treago Castle* attacks the ascent with the 9.15am Liverpool-Plymouth. On this occasion, the train seems well provided with first class accommodation; from the front there is a brake composite, a composite (both 'Toplights'), a third composite and a brake third. Two LM&SR coaches follow, the first of which may be an ex-L&NWR diner of the type seen closer to hand on page 16. *17th May 1934*

You may wonder why all that countryside to the right in this picture has been retained when, with little doubt, Norman Lockett would have excluded nearly all of it if making a print from his glass plate negative. Well, remember I mentioned in the acknowledgements of this book, my efforts (along with David Stubbs) to establish the exact locations of some of Norman's photographs, taken between Wellington and Whiteball Tunnel. Only one defeated us (and a local track worker we happened to meet) and this was it! However, logic suggests that the houses just visible across the fields and almost at right angles to the camera might be Rockwell Green, just a little to the west of Wellington. If so, nowadays some of the fields seen in the background are covered by the development known as Dobree Park, a part of the western expansion of Rockwell Green. The most prominent features hereabouts are two large water towers; an elderly brick structure and a concrete tower built circa 1930. I can only assume that, if I am correct as to the location, these 'distractions' were kept out of shot by Norman, in which case both would have been sited just beyond the right edge of this scene. Any reader who can confirm the location, please contact our publisher

NEAR BURRATOR

This proved to be a 'one-off' visit to the Princetown Branch by Norman, who photographed No. 4402 climbing away from Burrator Halt with an afternoon train, comprising a solitary clerestory brake composite coach providing 1st and 3rd class accommodation. Introduced as the '3101' Class in 1905 and later renumbered as the '44XX' Class, these small 2-6-2Ts with their 4ft 1½ins driving wheels were ideally suited to the steep gradients and serpentine curvature of this line, which ran from Yelverton for 10½ miles to reach Princetown, high up on Dartmoor. For many years, No. 4402 was regarded as the branch engine, out-stationed at the small engine shed at Princetown, generally only absent during boiler washouts and the like, when Laira usually substituted No. 4410. By the way, notice on the near side of No. 4402 the short, vertical, tubular-shaped fitting adjacent to the smokebox saddle. This was the reservoir of a wheel flange lubrication system fitted to reduce tyre wear. *20th June 1934*

No. 4402 featured in the local newspapers when, on 25th January 1939, she was derailed just outside Yelverton station. Setting off with the 4.51pm to Princetown against the starting signal and with the points still set for a dead-end siding, the locomotive ran through the buffers and plunged down an embankment. No. 4402 was raised on 3rd February 1939 and taken to Laira to await transfer to Swindon for repairs. The 2-6-2T returned to work the branch until withdrawn from service on 14th December 1949. The locomotive was cut up at Swindon during the 4-week period ending 12th August 1950, the first of the class to be scrapped.

PLYMOUTH LAIRA

On a Sunday in early May 1935, Norman Lockett paid a visit to the motive power depot at Laira. Although little more than a couple of miles from his home in Plymouth, this appears to have been his only visit to this large GWR depot which, no doubt. he found of little interest from a 'photogenic' point of view. Only three glass plates were exposed! Here we see one of the stud of 'Bulldog' 4-4-0s which were retained at Laira, certainly until the late 1940s and used, by this date, mostly for piloting duties on the South Devon banks. Although apparently not recorded by Norman, this is clearly No. 3427 (built as No. 3717 in 1906) which remained un-named until withdrawn from Laira in April 1938. *5th May 1935*

Inside the roundhouse at Laira, this array of tank engines includes a Class '1361' 0-6-0ST, designed and introduced in 1910 for shunting the dockside lines at Plymouth. Next in line is a '44XX' Class 2-6-2T, followed by two variants of the 0-6-0 pannier tank: a '2021' Class, which doubtless spent some of its time working the Sutton Harbour Branch, and a '64XX Class', many of which saw use in the Plymouth area, not least with the frequent railmotor services to and from Saltash. *5th May 1935*

To celebrate the centenary of the GWR in 1935, two locomotives were partially streamlined. In what was regarded as a project given less than whole-hearted support by CME C.B. Collett, only two locomotives were 'embellished', both of which remained in the condition seen here and opposite for only a short period. This side-on photograph of No. 6014 *King Henry VII* (the opposite side to all the official photographs I can recall having been published) was taken in June 1935, from a slightly elevated position providing a good clear view of the full extent of the modifications, including those enclosing the front top of the tender. The casings around the cylinders were the first to be removed, only a matter of weeks after No. 6014 was photographed here, waiting outside North Road station to take over an eastbound train. Notice the train identification number (a system introduced by the GWR the previous summer) had been chalked onto the front of the locomotive. The bullet nose was subsequently removed early in 1939 and by 1943 only the wedge-shaped front to the cab and the ventilation hatches to the cab roof survived as reminders of this rather inglorious episode.

The glass plate for this photograph has deteriorated to such an extent that it is no longer possible to obtain a satisfactory high resolution scan. Luckily, David had retained a print made many years ago, so this becomes the only image in the book that has been scanned from a print rather than directly from the glass plate.

The other locomotive selected to receive the 'streamline treatment' was No. 5005 *Manorbeir Castle*. Again the modifications were short-lived as, by the end of September 1935, the cowling over the front and the tender fairing had already been removed. During the summer of 1943 the remainder of the modifications were taken off (the locomotive regaining traditionally shaped nameplates), leaving only the wedged shape cab front, which survived until June 1947 (presumably removed during a Works visit to Swindon during May/June that year). No. 5005 was photographed by Norman Lockett shunting stock at North Road in May 1935 just a few weeks after the streamlining had been completed at Swindon. Careful study of this and the plate opposite reveals minor differences in the cowling ahead of the cylinders.

Just visible at the right extremity of this view is North Road East Signal Box. Built to replace the original box controlling the lines at this end of the station, it was brought into use in November 1908 and contained a 48 lever frame. Just a few years after featuring here in Norman's picture, this box, in turn, closed on 25th June 1939, to be replaced by a much larger East Box. The latter was provided in conjunction with the first phase of what was to become the much delayed rebuilding of North Road and its complex of lines.

MILLBAY AND MUTLEY

Class '4500' 2-6-2T No. 4548, of the earlier series with smaller straight top tanks, waits to leave Millbay station with the 5.25pm service to Tavistock. The large building seen in the background was (or, rather, is) the Duke of Cornwall Hotel, opened in 1862. Somehow, other than blast damage, it escaped the worst of the ravages of the Second World War and was later described by Sir John Betjeman, Poet Laureate, as one of the nation's finest examples of Victorian architecture. Threatened with demolition in the 1980s, fortunately it was saved and superbly restored. 26th June 1935

Note the enamel sign (extreme left) on the wall at the rear of the platform. Who can remember 'Burgoynes Tintara – A natural Tonic Wine with Restorative Powers'? The station, constructed by the South Devon Railway, was opened as Plymouth on 2nd April 1849. Ten years later, the Cornwall Railway commenced its services from here to Truro. On 28th March 1877, by which time ownership had passed to the GWR, the terminus was renamed Plymouth Millbay, shortly following the opening of North Road station. Millbay was closed to passenger traffic in late April 1941 (less than six years after Norman Lockett took this picture) when, suddenly, it became necessary to use the premises for goods traffic following the destruction of the adjacent goods depot during one of the numerous bombing raids on the city. The station remained in use for goods traffic until 1959, when the platforms were swept away to make way for new carriage sidings.

On a sunny Tuesday, 'Bulldog' No. 3342 *Bonaventura* and No. 6015 *King Richard III* are only just getting into their stride as they accelerate the 'Cornish Riviera Express' through Mutley station, having departed from North Road station little more than a minute earlier. The leading two coaches were the through portion from St. Ives, added at St. Erth. Perhaps something had gone awry as it was surprising to see an old clerestory brake composite on the 'CRE' by this date and normally under such circumstances, this would have been the leading vehicle. Notice also that, unlike all the other coaches, it is not carrying a roof board. *10th July 1934*

Situated almost within sight of North Road station, the suburban station of Mutley stood just to the west of the 183yd tunnel which takes the railway under Mutley Plain. The station, built by the South Devon Railway, pre-dated the opening of North Road by six years but was an early victim of the competing and ever-expanding network of local bus services. Mutley closed to traffic from 2nd March 1939. Close examination reveals that the brackets supporting the cast iron rainwater gutter along the front edge of the platform canopy were shaped as lions heads; a nice little detail to complement the ornate ironwork which supported the canopy and those superb lamps on the opposite platform!

NEAR CORNWOOD

'Star' Class 4-6-0 No. 4015 *Knight of St John* heads westwards, near Cornwood, with an afternoon Paddington to Plymouth train. This locomotive was one of a batch of ten constructed at Swindon in 1908 and all named after Knights. The leading coach looks as if it may be one of the 1929 wide-bodied 'Riviera' thirds, whilst the third coach is a 'Dreadnought' of 1905, the first type of GWR carriage to take advantage of the generous loading gauge afforded by the ex-broad gauge lines. *10th April 1936*

'Near Cornwood' was the only description Norman Lockett provided for this location, which he visited on a number of occasions. So here is another example of where some detective work proved necessary to establish the exact location which Norman had first visited in 1934. This task was made much easier by the inclusion of the signal which, it is reasonable to assume, would have been the Up Distant for either Ivybridge or, more likely, Cornwood Signal Box. But which? Neither David nor I had a clue! However, thanks to Chris Osment and his network of contacts I am able to confirm the signal as the Cornwood Up Distant which, of course, places this location as being near Venton, to the west of Cornwood station. Norman could have reached here from Plymouth either by bus – possibly alighting near Lee Mill followed by a lengthy walk – or, more likely, by train to Cornwood and a slightly shorter walk. Walking, however far, was no deterrent to Norman reaching the lineside in pursuit of his hobby. Indeed, whilst working our way through the collection of photographs, one of the things that has amazed both David and myself are those occasions when, it is apparent, Norman travelled (and walked) some considerable distance to reach a lineside, only then to take a single photograph. We thought at first this was, perhaps, the consequence of a sudden failure of his camera but, other than in the earliest years, invariably he carried two cameras both complete with glass plates. An only alternative (and an unlikely explanation), he was travelling somewhere else and made a diversion to the lineside just to get his one picture! No, on reflection, it was what David has referred to as his father's dogged determination and single minded approach to his hobby.

The same location a couple of months later, when Norman was able to take advantage of some evening sunshine to obtain this view of No. 5902 *Howick Hall*. Norman recorded the train as the 4.20pm goods from Newton Abbot, a Class 'K' service which, according to the time he noted as having taken the photograph, had thus taken 3¼ hours to cover a distance of only 24 miles from Hackney Yard. Notice, in the right background, a part of southern Dartmoor can be seen through the lineside fence, somewhere north of Wrangaton, near to where the main line reaches its highest altitute between Totnes and Plymouth. *10th June 1936*

'STAR' TURNS

'Star' Class No. 4072 *Tresco Abbey* heads away westwards from Aller Junction with an excursion from Bristol to Paignton. The row of cottages, seen in the background, was built by the railway and when I last passed along the adjacent A380 in 2009, was still standing, although most, if not all of the dwellings appeared to be empty, with the windows boarded. *17th May 1936* No. 4072, the last of the 'Stars' to be constructed, was released into traffic early in 1923 but remained in service less than two years beyond the date photographed here by Norman Lockett. The locomotive remains in as built condition, with the cylinders fed by internal steampipes, and thus makes an interesting comparison with the variants seen on the following two pages. After just fifteen years in service as a 'Star', No. 4072 was withdrawn and the frames and certain other parts re-used to construct 'Castle' Class No. 5092, the 'new' locomotive retaining the original name.

No. 4060 *Princess Eugenie* swings away from the Torbay line at Aller Junction and is about to commence the climb towards Dainton with the 9.10am Liverpool to Plymouth express. This locomotive received outside 'elbow pattern' steampipes when overhauled at Swindon towards the end of 1930. On this occasion, the train was comprised of a 'Toplight' brake composite, a brake third, another composite, an LM&SR coach, and a GWR brake third. *13th May 1936.*

The line from Aller Junction towards Torquay, Paignton and Kingswear, can be seen running on a slight embankment just two fields away in the right background. The main road runs parallel beyond the line but hidden behind the stone wall. Notice, by the way, in this and other pre-war photographs featuring this location, there is no Down Goods Loop between Aller Junction and the first overbridge reached along the main line towards Plymouth. This loop line was added during the Second World War.

We are now farther into the climb from Aller Junction towards Dainton Summit, at a location just in advance of the Down Distant signal for Stoneycombe, the tall wooden post and lower quadrant arm of which can be seen above the fourth coach of the train. 'Star' Class No. 4035 *Queen Charlotte* heads a 'boat special' from Paddington to Plymouth, Millbay Dock. Notice the leading coach; one of the 1932 'Super saloons' provided for first class travel on these trains, which were run especially for the ocean liner services calling at Plymouth Sound. *17th May 1936* No. 4035 was one of the 'Queen' series of ten 'Star' Class engines built during 1910-11, these being the first of the class to be superheated from new. This locomotive had been fitted with new cylinders fed by outside steampipes, a modification undertaken at Swindon at the start of 1931. Unlike No. 4060, seen on the previous page, these cylinders and steampipes were of a design similar to those fitted to the 'Castle' Class.

'Engine and two brakes'. On a bright September morning, Churchward 2-6-2T No. 4531 heads eastwards on the lower part of Hemerdon Incline with a pair of brake vans. *27th September 1936*
Were it not for knowing the mileage at this point (see page 53), it would be almost impossible to relate the backcloth to this picture to that which exists here today.

LITTLE
&
LARGE

In complete contrast, on an overcast day, No. 6022 *King Edward III*, ten minutes out from Plymouth North Road, storms the bank with the Up 'Cornish Riviera Limited'. Not, perhaps, the best of days to spend a few hours by the lineside but the immaculately prepared locomotive and the impressive exhaust certainly made up for the lack of sunshine. Notice the train is composed of the GWR 'Centenary' coaching stock, introduced on this service at the start of the summer service the previous year. *13th April 1936*
During the 1934-39 era, Norman Lockett invariably referred to the 'Cornish Riviera' using the suffix 'Limited' rather than 'Express'. Certainly, at the start of the summer service during the GWR centenary year, the train was renamed using 'Limited' but I remain unsure at what other periods this suffix, rather than 'Express', may have been used as part of the official title of this famous service.

NEAR HUTTON MOOR ROAD

In the summer of 1936, Norman Lockett took the first of his photographs to feature the area around his home town, Weston-super-Mare, to which he would return from Plymouth to live just four years later. These earliest photographs were taken (close to the family home) on the 'loop' which served the town, the exact location being about mid-distance between General and Locking Road stations, and Worle Junction, where the original Bristol-Taunton main line was regained.

The nearest West Country seaside town to the Midlands, Weston-super-Mare was, in the era before foreign package holidays became all the rage, always a popular choice for holiday makers from Birmingham and the Black Country. It was also a favourite with day excursionists living closer at hand – up to 75,000 visiting the resort on an August Bank Holiday during the mid 1930s, the vast majority of whom travelled to the town by rail. Nowadays, they nearly all come by car and, on a Bank Holiday weekend, you can often be in a queue for a couple of hours getting from the M5 the two miles into the town!

'Star' Class No. 4019 *Knight Templar* accelerates eastwards with the 10.15am Taunton to Paddington and is about to pass under the bridge which carries Hutton Moor Road across the line. David Lockett recalls that the tall building seen behind the train was the electricity works (the site of which has long since been redeveloped), located between the railway and the Locking Road. *8th July 1936*

It is curious how the first and last coaches look as if they could be in all-brown livery but this is probably an indication that they are due for a repaint! The second and fourth coaches are the first general purpose stock constructed with deep windows. They were known as 'Sunshine' coaches because the GWR extolled the use of 'Vita' glass, which is transparent to ultraviolet light – a tan before you even reached the seaside! Note how the standard height small windows in the coaches have their tops aligned with those of the large windows, leaving a cream band below the small windows. Unusually, the coach numbers, class and other lettering were all positioned on this cream band. This style of coach was used on 'The Bristolian' from its introduction in 1935 until the war.

As a child who sometimes spent the traditional week's summer holiday in Weston-super-Mare (a popular choice of my parents, the town being the nearest seaside resort to our home in west Wiltshire), I had assumed the title was something to do with it being a 'superior' seaside resort! Only later did I learn that the name Weston is made up of two Old English or Saxon words, meaning the west tun or settlement. Because there are several places called Weston in Somerset, descriptions were added to tell them apart. However, what is unusual about Weston-super-Mare is that the descriptive part of its name has remained in Medieval Latin. Super (with small 's') means on or above and mare is Latin for sea. (With acknowledgement to www.e-travelguide.info)

Seen at the same location but with Norman now standing to the side of Hutton Moor Road. No. 5026 *Criccieth Castle* is back to speed a mile after calling at Weston General station with a Kingswear to Cardiff train. At this date, the locomotive had only been in service from new for some twenty-seven months. The row of houses on the skyline fronts onto Locking Road, which runs parallel to the north of the railway for some distance eastwards out of the town. *8th July 1936*

To assist with identification of the many lineside locations visited by Norman Lockett around his home town, we have included a sketch map of the railways in this area on the next page and marked thereon some of the footpaths used by Norman to access the lineside. Much (indeed, most) of the area depicted in Norman's photographs as open countryside has been and continues to be built upon as various housing developments edge remorselessly ever farther east and southwards, away from the heart of the town.

We are now looking in an easterly direction, opposite to that seen in the views on the two previous pages. Weston Milton Halt (which had only opened three years earlier, on 3rd July 1933) can just be made out on the near side of the distant overbridge, which carries Locking Moor Road over the railway. This had been opened to serve the housing which was spreading out from the town centre along the Locking Road, which can be seen in the left background. 'Saint' Class 4-6-0 No. 2950 *Taplow Court* nears its destination with an excursion train bound for Locking Road station at Weston-super-Mare. *3rd August 1936*

Norman's negative has deteriorated and the inclusion of this photograph has only proved possible after much work to repair, as far as possible, most of the damage revealed when the plate was scanned. However, I wanted to include this one, not only because it includes a distant view of Weston Milton Halt but also the housing along Locking Road. Notice the young lad looking out from the first carriage; a railway enthusiast – or perhaps excited at the thought of spending some happy hours on the sands? No. 2950, built in 1912, was for many years allocated to Bristol, Bath Road shed, from where it was withdrawn on 29th September 1952.

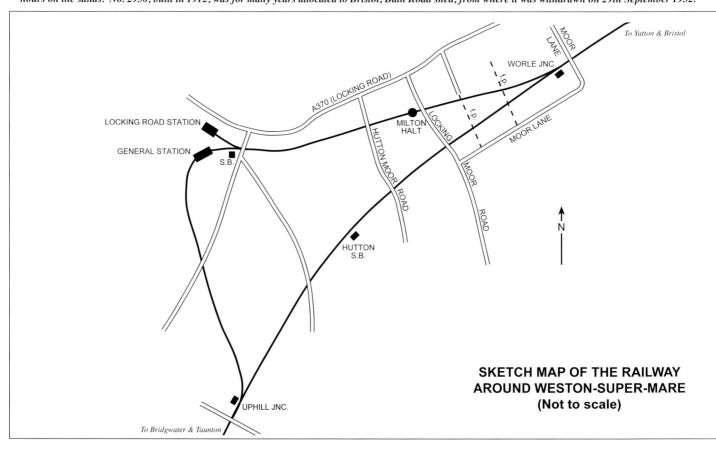

SKETCH MAP OF THE RAILWAY
AROUND WESTON-SUPER-MARE
(Not to scale)

Norman has now moved a little farther eastwards and to the opposite (north) side of the line, looking towards Weston Milton Halt; the access steps to the Down platform leading from Locking Moor Road can just be seen to the extreme left of this view. 'Star' Class No. 4022 *Belgian Monarch* is in charge of the 11.55am (Sundays) Crewe to Plymouth service. Norman recorded the passing time as 5.00pm. This train included portions that started from Manchester and Liverpool, and was remarshalled both at Newport and Bristol. The leading coach appears to have the small seat reservation letter boards towards each end, between the lavatory window and the next compartment. The fourth coach is probably a dining car. Notice, by the way, evidence here of the GWR's new policy of painting the casings of locomotive headlamps white instead of red, in order that they could be more easily seen by signalmen and linesmen. *16th May 1936*

The batch of ten 'Stars' No's 4021-30, built in 1909 and named after 'Kings', were destined to experience more than one change of title. No. 4022 was released into traffic as King William, the name carried until the '60XX' or 'King' Class was introduced in 1927, whereupon the locomotive was renamed as The Belgian Monarch. Later that same year, another change was made by omitting the word 'The'. Finally, in May 1940, the name was removed completely and No. 4022 ran thus until withdrawn on 14th February 1952.

NEAR UPHILL JUNCTION

Norman Lockett has now transferred his attention to the south-western end of the 'Weston Loop', where the Bristol-Taunton main line is regained at Uphill Junction, which lies behind his camera position here. 'Castle' Class No. 5084 *Reading Abbey* approaches the junction with the 4.40pm stopping train from Weston-super-Mare to Taunton. Released into traffic barely three months earlier and only recently reallocated to Bristol, Bath Road (supposedly after an initial few weeks at Weymouth), No. 5084 was a replacement for 'Star' Class No. 4064, from which the name was transferred, the first of a batch of ten such replacements during 1937, which re-used the frames of the original locomotives. *22nd June 1937*
The signal in the background was the Up Branch Starter for Uphill Junction which, in later years, was repositioned on the opposite side of the line to provide better sighting for footplate crews, as the Weston Branch swings sharply away from the main line.

Looking now in the opposite direction towards the junction (the signal box being just out of sight behind the trees on the extreme right of this view), 'Saint' Class No. 2939 *Croome Court* heads towards Weston with a Taunton to Bristol Temple Meads stopping train. *7th June 1938*
Built in December 1911, No. 2939 had been fitted with outside steam pipes eighteen months before being photographed here. The locomotive remained in use in this form until withdrawn from Bath Road shed on 6th December 1950.

SECTION 2
PRELUDE TO THE WAR YEARS

Norman Lockett could never have known at the time but his lineside visits during the final years leading up to the outbreak of the Second World War would prove to be the last of the truly independent days of the GWR. Long before the start of the war, the directors were, like all of the other 'Big Four' companies, becoming ever more concerned as to rising costs, not least the price of coal. One wonders, therefore, what the likes of Norman must have felt when news emerged that, in February 1938, the GWR had engaged consultants to investigate the economic advantages of electrifying the main line and branches westwards from Taunton. Was there,

perhaps, a collective sigh of relief amongst GWR enthusiasts when the consultants report concluded that the main line was not particularly suited to overhead electrification? The reasons given were the amount of curvature and other physical characteristics, the nature of the traffic (much of it seasonal) and the high cost of electric locomotives. The estimated cost, excluding most of the branch lines (already discounted by the consultants on economic grounds), would exceed £4 million (for 232 route miles) whilst the savings would amount to less than 1% of the capital expenditure. Consequently, the scheme was dropped in mid-1939.

No. 4022 *Belgian Monarch* features again. However, we have now moved south of Uphill Junction onto an area known as Bleadon Level. The overbridge seen here is the first south of Bleadon & Uphill station (closed 5th October 1964), and this Paddington to Taunton train had reached the commencement of a section of the main line which runs as straight as an arrow and all but level for mile after mile, through Brent Knoll, Highbridge, Dunball and on to Bridgwater. This train has four Collett, large window, coaches at the front, the first one being brand new and the second one being a 'Sunshine' type with the coach numbers on the cream band below the small windows. *15th June 1937*

This is an exposed area of the Somerset countryside to which Norman returned whenever he could find time during visits to his parents' home at Weston-super-Mare. Ideally located for an evening visit to the lineside and involving just a short bus or train ride, David recalls that lighting conditions could be quite challenging as the line ran all but due north-south and the evening sun often placed the front of the locomotive into shadow whereas one side of the train was brightly illuminated by the rays of the setting sun. David also remembers it as a place where the strong sou-westerly winds frequently blow unchallenged straight off the Bristol Channel, the shoreline of which is less than two miles distant!

Class '43XX' 2-6-0 No. 8337 trundles across the Level north of Brean Road Halt with a Class 'J' freight, which consists mostly of a large number of cattle trucks, possibly being worked back empty to service some of the (then) many West Country cattle markets. These trucks were also used in considerable numbers for the seasonal Cornish broccoli traffic. *15th June 1937*

Built in 1917, No. 8337 started out as No. 5337, an example of Churchward's very successful general purpose 'moguls' but was one of sixty-five of these locomotives in the '53XX' series which, during 1927/8, were modified. This was an attempt to minimise wear to the flanges of the leading coupled wheels, a problem which manifested itself particularly with locomotives of this class when working into Cornwall. The modification involved adding weight over the leading pair of wheels by inserting a heavy casting immediately behind the buffer plank – and this can be clearly seen in Norman's photograph. During 1944, this additional weight was removed from all but six of those still in service (twelve having been already withdrawn), whereupon each regained its original number. No. 8337 reverted to No. 5337 around October 1944. The few still numbered in the '83XX' range at the end of 1944 were similarly dealt with from early 1945 onwards.

LEAVING BREAN ROAD HALT

'Star' Class No. 5084 *Reading Abbey* pulls away from Brean Road Halt with the 4.40pm stopping train from Weston-super-Mare to Taunton. The Down side platform of the halt (opened in June 1929 and closed May 1955) can just be seen behind the train, immediately beyond the nearest overbridge carrying a minor road from Lympsham towards Brean Sands. *23rd June 1937*

The signal which can also be seen was controlled from Lympsham Signal Box, located on the Up side of the line between the two bridges in Norman's photograph but hidden from view. Taking its name from the nearby village, Lympsham Signal Box was provided in 1921 to break the 4½ mile section between Uphill Junction and Brent Knoll, and was closed on 21st December 1958.

BRENT KNOLL

With the Up Distant signal for Lympsham showing 'clear', No. 6000 *King George V* hurries across the levels with the 'North Mail', which included (from Plymouth) a TPO. Norman recorded the time as 6.45pm and arrival at Bristol Temple Meads was scheduled around 7.00pm. There, responsibility for hauling the train would pass to the LM&SR, with departure for Newcastle around 7.20pm. *15th June 1937.*

The hill prominent to the left is Brent Knoll which rises to a height of 449 feet and is the feature from which the next station to the south took its name. By the way, the glass plate from which this picture has been taken had been very badly marked by a stain caused by dampness. Much effort has been made to digitally remove the defect, as we wished to include the picture not only for its interest but because this is the only Up train to feature amongst a sequence of Down traffic.

'Bulldog' class 4-4-0 No. 3363 *Alfred Baldwin* passes with the 5.15pm semi-fast service from Bristol to Taunton. The interesting variety of stock comprises a Dean 40ft passenger brake van, a 70ft third class 'Dreadnought' and a 70ft 'Concertina', followed by what appears to be various Collett design coaches. *15th June 1937*

Class '28XX' 2-8-0 No. 2806, one of the first production batch of twenty of Churchward's heavy freight engines built in 1905, heads towards Highbridge with a local freight which was comprised mainly of wooden bodied open trucks. Notice how the exhaust is snatched away by the strong sou-westerly blowing across this very exposed section of the main line at Brean Level. *23rd June 1937*

SOMERSET/DEVON MAIN LINE 1937-38

We now take you down the main line from Norman's home town, returning towards Plymouth where he continued to live and work until 1940. The locations visited were limited in number, some warranting only a single photograph (possibly taken during a change of train), others which became favourites and to which Norman returned many times.

'Star' No. 4022 *Belgian Monarch* was obviously a regular as here she is again! Photographed at Taunton station from the island platform serving the Up and Down through lines, No. 4022 is preparing to leave with the 11.20am stopping train to Bristol Temple Meads. By the way, notice how neat and tidy everything was kept – I'll wager that sheet of newspaper was retrieved and binned before too many more hours had passed! How times have changed. *21st June 1937*
I mentioned earlier how this locomotive's name was removed from May 1940. This was following the wartime invasion of Belgium earlier that same month. Thereafter, No. 4022 bore only the legend 'Star Class' painted on the central wheel splashers. This photograph is the only example David has found in the collection so far to feature this important station. David informed me that his father, when returning from a visit to Weston-super-Mare to his home in Plymouth, would sometimes catch a 'stopper' as far as Taunton and change there into a 'fast' to Plymouth. He also used Taunton to change from train to bus if – as on this occasion – intending to visit the lineside around Whiteball.
At the time when Norman took the photograph above, the rebuilding of Taunton station had been completed only five years earlier. These substantial works included the provision of the central island platforms. This resulted in a platform face for each of the four through lines, which the GWR had laid down between Cogload, to the east, and Norton Fitzwarren, to the west. Following the closure of the branch lines which were served by trains to and from Taunton – to Yeovil via Langport West, Chard Junction via Ilminster, and Barnstaple via Dulverton – the central island platforms were stripped bare around 1967 and, other than in an emergency, became unused. At the start of 1971, the line to Minehead succumbed as well. However, changing fortunes in rail traffic resulted in the two island platforms being brought back into use in 2000. Subsequently, some covered waiting accommodation was provided to these same platforms and, much more recently, a new lift has been installed. All of which, no doubt, was provided at great cost and serves as but one illustration of the countless follies authorised during that era when, nationwide, the railway infrastructure was callously reduced to a minimum – and that's the nearest this tome gets to making a political statement!

SOUTH OF BEAM BRIDGE

On a lovely sunny afternoon (the time recorded as 3.05pm), Stafford Road based No. 5031 *Totnes Castle* passes milepost 172½ with the 10.40am Wolverhampton to Penzance express. Although Norman made no mention of it, there appears to be a plume of exhaust at the rear of this train; a banker – or was it a lineside fire? *21st June 1937*

The location featured here is less than a quarter mile south of Beam Bridge, where the main line climbs at 1 in 80 to the mouth of Whiteball Tunnel, just short of another mile farther south. The milepost shows the distance as measured by the original 'Great Way Round' (via Bath and Bristol). The mileage from Paddington via the Patney to Creech route but excluding the later Westbury/Frome avoiding lines was about 20¼ miles less. Notice how the local gang has cut a swath of the grass along the side of the ballast.

With this North to West express comprising a loading of only 'seven', the climb to Dainton would not present the combined efforts of No. 3449 *Nightingale* and No. 4074 *Caldicot Castle* with a serious challenge! After all, this was the same 'Castle' selected by the GWR for tests in 1924 and, the following year, for comparative trials *(during which it performed rather well!)* against L&NER Gresley Class 'A1' Pacific No. 4474 *Victor Wild*. Built in December 1909 (as number 3739 and later renumbered), No. 3449 was one of the 'Bird' series which represented the final development of the 'Bulldog' class 4-4-0s. *18th May 1937*

ALLER JUNCTION

Norman's first photograph to feature one of the versatile and popular 'Grange' Class. Just nine months from new, Laira-based 4-6-0 No. 6801 *Aylburton Grange*, having negotiated Aller Junction, gathers some speed to attack the start of the climb to Dainton Summit with the 4.20pm goods from Newton Abbot. The train is assisted in the rear by a large 2-6-2T, attached at Newton Abbot because this view pre-dates the provision of the Down Goods Loop, which would be installed at Aller during the Second World War. *18th May 1937*

From Aller Junction, approximately the first quarter-mile towards Totnes is downhill before the start of the climb towards the summit at Dainton is reached. After the Down Goods Loop was installed, a freight service pausing here for a banker lost any advantage to be gained from this initial – albeit brief – favourable grade. No. 6801 was fitted, when first released into traffic, with a tapered cast iron chimney, a feature only applied to the first four of these locomotives. By the date of Norman's photograph, this had already been replaced with a new pattern copper-capped chimney.

CONTRASTING TRAFFIC NEAR CORNWOOD

Two scenes of contrasting traffic on the climb towards Ivybridge, about a mile to the east of Cornwood, both taken during the afternoon of Wednesday, 13th April 1938. The weather conditions look different, as a late afternoon haze had formed by the time Norman took the picture below. *(See captions opposite)*

A WINDY DAY AT HEMERDON!

On a bright but very blustery day, 'Bulldog' Class 4-4-0 No. 3453 *Seagull* and 4-6-0 No. 5011 *Tintagel Castle* fight their way up the final section of the bank towards Hemerdon Up Distant signal. The heavy train was conveying passengers from New York, who had disembarked into GWR tenders in Plymouth Sound from the Cunard liner *Queen Mary*, which had made her maiden voyage less than a year earlier. No. 5011 was a little older, built at Swindon in 1927, whilst No. 3453 dated back to 1910. *29th March 1937*
This photograph is presented here much as Norman himself would have printed it, to concentrate the eye on the locomotives and the spectacular smoke and steam effects. However, as the distant signal cropped out on the right features in several other views he took here, we didn't think it would matter in this instance.

OPPOSITE PAGE TOP: A reminder of when the GWR carried large quantities of Cornish vegetables – which, because of the southerly climate tended to crop earlier than similar produce from other parts of the country – to the markets in London and the Midlands. No. 4076 *Carmarthen Castle* heads eastwards with a Class 'C' express freight, which Norman recorded as an 'Up broccoli' train. No. 4076 was, at the time, based at Exeter.

OPPOSITE PAGE BOTTOM: The 'North Mail', which started out as the 12.30pm from Penzance and conveyed LM&SR, in addition to GWR, stock. The motive power, from Plymouth, is provided by 'Bulldog' Class 4-4-0 No. 3453 *Seagull* assisting 4-6-0 No. 6022 *King Edward III*.
For modellers, we have included this view because of the stock, which has been identified by John Lewis. The leading vehicle is a Collett period mail van, possibly 799 or 800, from Plymouth to Bristol; the second and third are from either Penzance or Plymouth to Bristol, the third vehicle appearing to be a 70ft coach (which would not be allowed to travel off GWR metals). The fourth, in clean brown nord cream livery, is a brake composite, followed by two Siphon Gs, all from Penzance to Liverpool. Next there are three LM&SR coaches, a passenger brake van, a composite and a brake third, from Penzance to Manchester. These are followed by a GWR brake composite from Plymouth to Glasgow, another Siphon G, and at least two more vehicles which cannot be identified. How's that for variety!

LOWER HEMERDON – 2

We are back at the lineside on the lower half of Hemerdon Incline but, as mentioned earlier, Norman took so many photographs here we are seriously spoilt for choice! No. 4093 *Dunster Castle* ascends the incline with the 10.30am (Sundays) Plymouth to Paddington express. *17th April 1938*

I have made reference earlier of my trying to establish the exact location of some of Norman's earliest photographs. This has been part of the enjoyment in putting together this book. All of Norman's photographs taken here were described by him merely as 'Hemerdon Bank', a degree of vagueness which, doubtless, proved more than sufficient for him to recall many years later exactly the whereabouts of this particular location on the bank. As is all too evident, in the 1930s (and, indeed, until a much later era) this section of Hemerdon Bank – although only some five miles east from Plymouth North Road station – was out 'in the sticks'. Today, however, much of the once green and pleasant backdrop seen here is well and truly urbanised, having succumbed to both residential and commercial developments on the eastern side of Plympton.

Six weeks earlier, a sunny Sunday morning in early April must have proved an irresistible opportunity to Norman to head out to Hemerdon for an hour or so! Here, he was rewarded with a credibly clean 4-6-0, No. 4957 *Postlip Hall*, **bustling up the incline with the lightly-loaded 11.10am(Sundays) Plymouth Millbay to Newton Abbot train which, a few minutes earlier, had made its customary call at Plympton station.** *6th March 1938*
The leading carriage appears to be a GWR clerestory corridor composite. Originally fitted with gas lighting, there appear to be battery boxes suggesting the coach had been converted to electric lighting. Beyond the two Collett coaches, another clerestory brings up the rear.

Bristol-based 4-6-0 No. 4951 *Pendeford Hall* heads the 9.45am (Sundays) Plymouth-Paddington, which ran via Bristol and arrived at its final destination at 4.10pm. No. 4951 possibly worked the service as far as Bristol. For those in the 'know', by waiting at Plymouth for the 10.30am (Sundays) train, which took the direct line via Castle Cary, one could reach Paddington thirty minutes earlier than by taking the 9.45am! *20th March 1938*

Apparently, on Sundays, almost any stock might be used on this train. Here, we have two old corridor clerestory thirds at the head, followed by a 70ft dining car which had been modernised – it had been given large windows with sliding ventilators in the passenger saloon. The three coaches behind the diner had formed the 7.20pm Penzance to Plymouth (North Road) the previous evening. If you have read my comments opposite, you will realise why the discovery of this photograph left me a little frustrated. Norman had moved just a matter of a few feet eastwards from the position he usually took up here but it proved sufficient to reveal his exact whereabouts – milepost 241!

With scenes such as those reproduced on these pages, one can appreciate only too readily why Norman found this location on Hemerdon Incline so much to his liking. A short bus ride and walk from his home, the variety of hard working steam, much of it in tandem, an attractive rural backcloth – what more could he want! Of course, all these many years later, the pictures also provide a fascinating record of the almost endless variety of coaching stock which the GWR employed, not that this feature would have influenced Norman as to whether or not he should expend another glass plate! Variety, however, is not something today's enthusiasts are blessed with.

ABOVE: One of the first series of the ubiquitous 'Hall' Class, 1929-built No. 4943 *Marrington Hall* is seen here coupled ahead of 'Mogul' No. 8350 with the 7.45am Penzance to the North of England service. *12th May 1937*
This was another of the Churchward '53XX' Class modified in 1927-8 to redistribute the weight but later reinstated (during 1944) to its earlier condition and regaining its original number 5350. The locomotive was, for many years, allocated to Newton Abbot.

LEFT: I included this photograph of a 'Castle' Class in charge of what looks like a local service some time during 1936, because Norman had climbed the side of the shallow cutting on the Down side of the line and this provides a better view of the countryside. The first four coaches are all Collett designed 'high waist' vehicles; the last coach is not clear enough to identify. I am unable to tell you with certainty the details of the motive power as the original envelope in which the glass plate negative was kept (and on which Norman wrote such information) has been lost and replaced with a blank envelope. Anyway, for any reader who lives or works in the eastern outskirts of Plympton, to the north of the main line, this is how it used to look! The row of large trees prominent above the train stretched across to the lineside near to the location of the Down Distant signal for Plympton. Notice also several examples of a once familiar countryside feature, the hayrick, invariably built at one side or corner of a field. Each rick was temporarily fenced off to deter the attention of any cattle or other farm stock using the same field to graze. Most ricks, as here, were also 'topped out' with straw thatch to fend off the worst of the elements. All so much more pleasing to the eye than those huge, round, black plastic covered hay bales which are the norm nowadays.
As regards the identity of the locomotive, my money here would be on No. 5016 Montgomery Castle *which, during 1936, was allocated first at Newton Abbot, then to Penzance. The design of the inside cylinder front casings and wider cab-front window would tie in with my choice and the scan when enlarged reveals what might be a couple of the appropriate numerals on the buffer plank. (By the way, I wouldn't want readers to be overly impressed by my supposed detailed knowledge of the 'Castle' class – it's all available in* The Book of the Castle 4-6-0s, *published by Irwell Press!)*

'Prairie' tank No. 5531 swings away from the main line at Tavistock Junction and rounds the curve near Marsh Mills with the 6.10pm from Plymouth Millbay to Launceston, a journey which occupied a few minutes over an hour and a half. Until closure to passenger traffic in late April 1941, the terminus at Millbay was the starting or finishing point for services via the Launceston Branch, which opened as far as Tavistock in 1859 and to Launceston in 1865. *19th August 1936*

The stock used to form this train looks rather like a scratch set. From the front there is a clerestory brake third attached the 'wrong' way round, a 10-compartment third of 1905, a clerestory lavatory composite and a relatively new brake third. I wonder if the clerestory coaches were more comfortable than the (then) more recent examples?

LAUNCESTON BRANCH TRAFFIC

Devoting most of what little time he could spare to visits to the main line, Norman Lockett did not entirely overlook the branch line scene – but such visits were comparatively rare. Whilst living in Plymouth, the obvious choice for a dedicated enthusiast of GW steam was the local line to Tavistock and Launceston, which he could reach either by bus or train. Clearbrook Halt had been provided less than ten years before Norman paid a first visit. No doubt the very picturesque countryside hereabouts was the reason he made several subsequent visits for, as was often

the case, once he had discovered a good location for photography, he rarely ventured farther to find others!

This trait by Norman (and, seemingly, several other of his contemporaries from this era) to return time and time again to the same lineside location rather than explore other possibilities nearby, I find difficult to understand. However, David has pointed out it was the quality and composition of the finished photograph which mattered most to his father, who would return to the same location in his determination always to improve on previous efforts.

No. 4598, one of the later series '45XX's with the larger capacity, slope-top side tanks, hussles along the branch with the 5.25pm Millbay to Tavistock. We think this location, which Norman described only as '*near Clearbrook*' is between Shaugh Bridge Platform and Clearbrook Halt. That would tie in with the time the photograph was taken as recorded by Norman. *1st June 1937*

The 5.25pm Millbay to Tavistock was booked to employ a 'B Set', two non-corridor brake composites with their brake ends outwards, usually permanently coupled. However, this is a four coach train with a non-corridor brake third and a third class leading. Unfortunately the rear two coaches cannot be identified. It is hard to imagine that this idyllic line had witnessed not only the broad gauge locomotives and stock of the South Devon Railway (later part of the GWR) but also, for fourteen years from May 1876, the Plymouth traffic of the L&SWR, during which time, to accommodate this, the line between Marsh Mills and Lydford was mixed gauge. This was before that company gained independent access via the Plymouth, Devonport & South Western Junction Railway's line from Lydford to Devonport.

Nowadays, this section of the old railway line forms a part of the popular Plym Valley Cycle Route, which extends from the grounds of Saltram House, alongside the Plym Estuary, as far north as Clearbrook. On the way, you will pass the Plym Valley Railway, a heritage line which shares the section of the former GWR route between Marsh Mill and Lee Mill Crossing. Operating dates are shown on the railway's website www.plymrail.co.uk

A foretaste of Spring was in the air when Norman returned to the Launceston Branch to capture this superb picture, again near Clearbrook. This train, the 3.05pm from Plymouth Millbay, worked the full length of the line to Launceston and 2-6-2T No. 4502, hauling a two-coach 'B' set, make up a classic Great Western branch line scene. Originally No. 2163, this locomotive was one of the first three lots totalling twenty engines, built at Wolverhampton during 1906-08 – the last locomotives to be constructed there before all new-build was consolidated at Swindon. The outside steam pipes were a later modification. *4th March 1938*

PASSING TRERULE FOOT

There can be little doubt that Norman took a liking to this location because, in the evening, the lighting could be perfect for photographing Down trains. Indeed, it appears he never took a single picture here looking in the opposite direction at any time of the day! No. 4901 *Adderley Hall* returns towards its home shed at Penzance with the 10.32am (SX) through train from Crewe. Here, the train, running well to time according to Norman's note, heads past Trerule Foot and towards its first call within Cornwall at Liskeard, timed for 6.33pm. The onward journey to Penzance would take a little over two more hours to complete. *20th July 1937*

Nowadays, the pattern of small individual meadows seen hereabouts has been altered beyond all recognition, with so many hedgerows swept away to create the large single enclosures which typify the modern rural scene.

Grass cutting for haymaking had commenced in the field adjoining the Down side of the line at Trerule Foot, enabling Norman to obtain this fine view. Notice the farmer had left his mowing machine – a horse-drawn model (possibly a 'Bamford') – ready to complete cutting the field. Perhaps the task of afternoon milking had intervened. At 5.20pm, No. 4947 *Nanhoran Hall* sweeps westwards with the 10.40am (SX) Wolverhampton to Penzance, running to time towards Liskeard, the first scheduled stop after leaving North Road station. *20th July 1937*

Notice the composition of the train. The leading coach is a brake composite in the 'large window' style. Coach two is a brake third, coach three a 'Sunshine' type third (note the large windows and the way the droplights etc. have an area of cream below them). Coach four is the dining car, followed by a composite and a brake third. The last two vehicles are a composite and a brake third, both destined for Newquay. The leading brake composite returned northwards next day on the 7.45am Penzance to Crewe, as far as Bristol, where it was transferred to the 2.15pm to Wolverhampton. Coaches two to six (above) also returned from Penzance next morning but on the 10.40am to Wolverhampton. This train also collected, at Par, the returning two rear coaches – just one example of the often complex utilisation of GWR coach workings.

TWO ROUTES FROM ALLER

A return to the trackside near Aller, this time to the Torbay line. Norman had obviously reached the lineside via the first overbridge south of the junction, which carries a lane over the railway. Notice the small lineside orchard with the trees in blossom. Locally based No. 4077 *Chepstow Castle* heads an afternoon local from Newton Abbot to Kingswear. Norman recorded the time as 4.10pm, so it is likely that this was the 4.05pm Newton Abbot to Kingswear. This train was due to be formed of a brake third and a composite off the 10.40am from Wolverhampton, plus two three coach sets, one of which was used for the 5.40pm Kingswear to Exeter and the other the 6.36pm Kingswear to Taunton. The first and third coaches are deep window 'Sunshine' types of 1936, the rest appear to be standard Collett 'high waist' types of 1922-35. Many years later, during the early BR era, much needed additional stabling sidings were provided between Paignton and Goodrington, thus relieving the limited capacity available at Paignton. *10th May 1938*

From the overbridge referred to in the previous caption, it's just a few minutes walk along the lane to reach the corresponding first bridge (Langford Bridge) south-west of Aller Junction on the main line to Plymouth. Exeter-based No. 6814 *Enborne Grange* had yet to make eighteen months in service when photographed here, heading what Norman referred to only as a 'North to West' express. The time was 5.30pm but the only train which might fit Norman's description was the 10.32am Crewe to Plymouth, scheduled to depart Newton Abbot just after 5pm. However, if it is that train (there running nearly 30 minutes late), why has a large fish van, code name 'Bloater', been added to the front and why, apparently, has the dining car been removed and an extra coach added to the rear of what would be the usual formation of the train? Incidentally, this date was a Tuesday and, assuming we have identified the train correctly as the 10.32am from Crewe, the rather ancient passenger brake van (second vehicle) was one of the GWR Hotels Department's 'Refreshment vans'. *10th May 1938*

The 'Grange' Class, first introduced in 1936 and utilising parts from withdrawn Class '43XX' 'Moguls', proved a very suitable mixed traffic design for use on the South Devon banks and throughout the West Country, with their excellent steaming and hill-climbing abilities. No. 6814 spent many years based first at Exeter, then Newton Abbot, and – I believe – was never allocated farther east than Bristol.

Now back near the summit of Hemerdon Incline for a final couple of pictures taken close to the Up Distant signal. Norman recorded No. 5017 *St Donats Castle* in charge of a Plymouth-Goodrington excursion. The timing of the photograph suggests the train may have been running in the path of the Plymouth-Paignton excursion, a 'dated' service (*see page 77 for details*). The train appears to include two passenger brake vans – the leading coach and, apparently, the penultimate one. There are two clerestory coaches (the fourth and the last), otherwise seven relatively modern Collett 'high waist' coaches have been provided, probably all third class only. *17th July 1938*

The large numerals carried on the front of the smokebox of No. 5017 were an example of the new system of train identification first introduced by the GWR in 1934. The numbering sequence adopted for express services starting from the various operating districts was as follows: Paddington 100-199; Shrewsbury 200-299; Wolverhampton & Birmingham 300-399; Bristol 400-499; Exeter 500-599; Plymouth 600-699; and South Wales 700-799. Special trains and boat trains were supposed to carry the number '0' in the left-hand slot but, as witnessed here (and in other views), invariably this was omitted. The numerals, 16 inches high and, it was claimed, easily identifiable from a ¼ mile distant, were painted onto thin plates, which were slotted into a frame attached to the front of the smokebox. The number of each train ended 0 or 5 with other numbers used when a train was run in more than one part. The Down 'Cornish Riviera Express' was allocated '125' and any division of this train '126' to '129'. In the opposite direction the Up 'Riviera' was allocated '615'.

A rather overcast Sunday morning in May finds Norman again near the summit at Hemerdon to take just this single photograph. The train is the 10.30am (Sundays) Plymouth-Paddington express, with motive power supplied by No. 4940 *Ludford Hall*. Norman recorded the time as 10.50am, so the train was about 2 minutes down on schedule; not a problem with this loading as, given a clear run, generally time could be made up before reaching the first scheduled stop at Newton Abbot. *22nd May 1938*

This location was reached by Norman via the overbridge carrying Ledgate Lane, close to the top of the 1 in 42 climb and the easing of the gradient before Hemerdon Signal Box was reached. The copse abutting the Up side boundary is still recognisable in 2010.

FINAL PRE-WAR BRANCH LINE VISITS

We believe this location to be about mid-distance between Shaugh Bridge Platform and Clearbrook Halt, north of Shaugh Tunnel and where a narrow road ran parallel with the course of the Launceston Branch for a short distance. It was a very attractive location; just the sort of remote and unspoilt spot which appealed to Norman Lockett. The train is the 4.30pm from Plymouth Millbay to Yelverton, with motive power provided by 2-6-2T No. 4598. *14th June 1938*

The 4.30pm from Plymouth to Yelverton was scheduled to be formed of a Plymouth Division three coach 'E Set' 'strengthened as necessary'. However, here we have a train of four clerestory coaches – three 8-compartment thirds and what appears to be a recently repainted brake composite.

Nearly a year after taking the previous photograph, 0-6-0PT No. 9770 is seen climbing through the woods near Clearbrook. Again, the train is the 4.30pm from Millbay to Yelverton. *23rd May 1939*

Built at Swindon in 1936, No. 9770 was allocated first to Taunton, then to Laira. In later years, the locomotive was transferred to BR Southern Region, appearing first at Waterloo on empty coaching stock workings in December 1958. Having been tested on the Folkestone Harbour line, it was reported as having made a brief foray back to the West Country for tests on the Wadebridge-Bodmin North services during April 1959. No. 9770 ended her days transferred back to WR stock at Bath Green Park in July 1963 and withdrawn from there at the start of December that year. Whether turning a wheel at Bath in revenue-earning traffic or merely stored pending withdrawal, I have yet to determine.

Looking absolutely magnificent, the spotless condition of No. 5062 *Tenby Castle* (ignore that one stain down the boiler cladding!) is explained by the fact that the locomotive may not yet have been formally released into traffic. Indeed, this must have been within its first few days in use, as No. 5062 was the third of six 'Castles' completed at Swindon in June 1937 and the mid-point of the month had only just been passed when Norman took this photograph during an early-evening visit to Bristol Temple Meads. The first recorded allocation was to Stafford Road on or around the 23rd of the month. *17th June 1937.*

WHAT'S IN A NAME? – 1

The photograph opposite is probably one of very few of No 5062 whilst bearing the name *Tenby Castle*. Just a month later, a decision was made by the GWR to rename all fifteen of the class constructed during 1936, plus all six built in 1937. The origins of the new names carried by these 'Castles' was as follows. During 1936, the names of 'Earls' were allocated to the (then) recently rebuilt locomotives which combined the boilers designed for the 'Duke' or '3252' Class 4-4-0s (dating from 1895) with the frames, cylinders and coupled wheels as used for the 'Bulldog' Class. Of the resultant hybrids, No. 3219 was to be given the name *Earl of Shaftesbury*. However, in 1937, with only the first thirteen rebuilds yet carrying a name, the decision was made to abandon the exercise and remove those already in use, allocating the 'Earl' names instead to the 1936-7 built 'Castles' (hope you've all followed that!). Just to complete the story, the now nameless 'Earls', as a reflection of their origins, became known (unofficially but readily adopted) as the 'Dukedogs' and, in 1946, were renumbered as the '90XX' series. It's been recorded that the change of heart by the GWR in 1937 was the consequence of some of those Earls of the Realm, the names of whom had been selected (some of whom were also directors of the GWR), having not been over-enamoured at the thought of their titles being carried on such ancient looking engines as the new 'hybrids'. Doubtless those concerned were much better disposed to see their title appended to a 'Castle'!

In early November 1937, barely five months after release into traffic as *Tenby Castle*, No. 5062 was renamed *Earl of Shaftesbury*. Norman Lockett photographed the locomotive again (but now carrying its new name) near Aller Junction, in charge of the 6.04pm departure from Newton Abbot, a stopping service to Plymouth. By this date No. 5062 had been transferred to Newton Abbot. *10th May 1938*
This train was due to be formed of an 'E Set' (non-corridor brake composite, lavatory third, brake third) plus two corridor thirds. The corridor thirds are the two leading clerestory coaches but instead of the standard 'E Set', there is a three year old 'Sunshine' coach, a clerestory brake third and a clerestory composite, probably all corridor coaches. These three coaches worked to a three day cycle, mostly in South Devon, but including a return journey to Taunton and another to Liskeard, which may be the reason why corridor coaches were being used. Moretonhampstead and Kingswear were also visited.

IVYBRIDGE AND CORNWOOD

What Norman Lockett's great friend from a later era, Ivo Peters, would have called a 'worm's eye view', aptly describes this scene of a Down express west of Ivybridge. *Summer 1938*
The original envelope onto which Norman would have written the details of his negative has, we suspect, been lost because the glass plate now resides inside a blank envelope! However, as this location features so seldom in Norman's collection, we wished to include it here. Unfortunately, the final digit of the number on the buffer beam is too indistinct to read but the first three are '502' so this might well be Laira-based No.5021 Whittington Castle.

PASSING MILEPOST 236½

East of Cornwood, No. 5043 *Earl of Mount Edgcumbe* heads towards Ivybridge with the 1.20pm (Sundays) Plymouth-Paddington express. Until the previous September (when still only eighteen months from new), No. 5043 had carried the name *Barbury Castle*. This nine coach train has a 70ft composite as the second coach with a dining car behind. Otherwise it is all third class accommodation. The penultimate coach is a 70ft 'Dreadnought' of 1905. *21st August 1938*

Milepost 236½ reveals this location to be near the hamlet of Fardell, just over a mile east of Cornwood station and nearly mid-distance towards Ivybridge. Norman's visit here, being on a Sunday, suggests he caught the bus from Plymouth along the A38 as far as Lee Mill and then walked the minor road towards Cornwood, in order to reach this location.

At the same location, the following May, the 2.15pm (SX) Plymouth-Exeter stopping train is hauled by Bath Road based No. 4096 *Highclere Castle* and Laira-based No. 4932 *Hatherton Hall*. A case of 'ANR' (assistance not required) with the 'Castle', no doubt, attached to avoid a separate light engine movement – perhaps as far as Newton Abbot, where this all stations service was scheduled to wait for 39 minutes before resuming the run eastwards. *29th May 1939*

A mid-afternoon in May provided this delightful scene, with 4-4-0 No. 3453 *Seagull* heading eastwards, in charge of a lightweight Class 'C' freight conveying cattle and perishables traffic. Notice the embankment on the Down side of the line bedecked with wild flowers. Norman recorded the conditions as 'bright sunshine' but the manner in which the exhaust is being swept away suggests quite a stiff wind was blowing off the southern slopes of Dartmoor! The exhaust partially obscuring the side of the locomotive is possibly the reason why Norman appears never to have made a print from his negative. *29th May 1939*

No. 3453 was one of the 'Bird' series, the final version of the 'Bulldogs' comprising fifteen locomotives built in 1909 and (as in the case of No. 3453) 1910. Seagull, together with No. 3454 Skylark were the last of the class to be withdrawn, both from Reading shed in early-November 1951 and taken to Swindon for cutting up.

Having spent some of the morning of August Bank Holiday Monday at Hemerdon, Norman next made his way to the eastern end of Blackford Viaduct. Cornwood station was situated just beyond the far end of this impressive structure, which carries the main line on a sweeping curve high above the River Yealm, here just a few miles from its source on the southern side of Dartmoor. Norman had taken a position farther away from the lineside than was his usual preference, in order to include in the frame as much of the impressive structure as he could, whilst managing to avoid, as far as possible, the telegraph wires which crossed the valley by means of insulators attached to the side of the viaduct. This splendid image shows No. 6019 *King Henry V*, with the Up 'Cornish Riviera Express', climbing towards Ivybridge and the summit near Wrangaton. With the exception of the second and fifth coaches, the train is made up from the 'Centenary' stock, although the original wind-down windows have been replaced with fixed panes incorporating Airstream ventilators (installed between 1936-8). The wooded backdrop makes for an even better composition on what had become rather overcast conditions. *7th August 1939*

In this more conventional view of the viaduct, No. 6007 *King William III* speeds eastwards with the Up relief to the 'Cornish Riviera Express' running just 5 minutes ahead of the main train seen in the previous photograph. Here, Norman was able to take advantage of the last of the sunshine just before the skies clouded over. *7th August 1939*
This seven coach relief has only two of the special 'Centenary' coaches built for the 'CRE', immediately behind the locomotive, followed by what is probably a two-car dining set, a couple of 70ft 'Toplight' coaches and a Collett 'high waist' brake third.

BLACKFORD VIADUCT

LOWER HEMERDON – 3: FINAL PRE-WAR VISITS

Laira-based 2-8-0 No. 4703 is given a run with what Norman recorded as a Plymouth-Exeter excursion, here storming up Hemerdon Incline. *9th July 1939*
Norman noted the time as 10.20am, so this must have been a train running in the same path as the 9.55am (SX) Saltash to Exeter – a summer holiday service shown in the Working Time Table as running for four weeks only from late July. Having collected the motley variety of coaching stock from the sidings at Wearde (west of Saltash), the train called at every station and halt on the short journey towards North Road, then ran non-stop to Newton Abbot. There, on weekdays other than the August Bank Holiday week, carriages for Paignton were dropped off. The main train continued eastwards, calling only at Teignmouth and Dawlish before terminating at Exeter. Similar arrangements were in hand for the return journey which terminated at Saltash at 8.07pm; the empty stock then tripped out to the sidings at Wearde. Whilst the first two coaches are modern Collett large-window types, the next four may well be LM&SR stock, whilst the rearmost coach looks to be a 'Dreadnought'.

OPPOSITE PAGE BOTTOM: Another visit was made to Blackford Viaduct the following Sunday. 'Bulldog' 4-4-0 No. 3426 and a 'King' Class (which Norman noted as 'probably' No. 6001 *King Edward Vll*) power across the masonry arches with what Norman recorded as the 2.50pm (Sundays) Plymouth-Paddington express. However, looking at the Service Time Table for summer 1939, no such train is listed! According to the time Norman noted against his photograph, this is possibly the 1.00pm (Sundays) Newquay-Paddington, which departed Plymouth at 3.00pm and was about seven minutes down on schedule. The WTT contained a note stating that the leading locomotive was to work through as far as Newton Abbot (where this service was not booked to call) when assistance was required beyond Hemerdon. *13th August 1939*
This very heavy train is a good example of what the GWR might muster when pressed at peak summer holiday weekends. The leading coach is a 69ft brake composite (originally a tri-composite) of 1905 and one of the last GWR coaches to be built with guards lookout. This is followed by a 'Dreadnought' of a similar length and vintage; then come a 'Centenary' brake third and another coach from the 'CRE'. The fifth coach was a 'Toplight', followed by a three coach dining car set, whilst those second and third from the rear of the train are 70ft 'Toplights'. How's that for variety.

No. 3446 *Goldfinch*, one of a group of locomotives built in 1909-10, representing the final development of the 'Bulldog' Class 4-4-0s (sometimes referred to as the '3441' or 'Bird' Class), assists No. 6001 *King Edward VII* up Hemerdon Incline with the 10.30am (Sundays) Plymouth to Paddington express. *13th August 1939*

The 'Bulldog' 4-4-0s retained a long association with this section of the West of England main line, a number being allocated, for example, to Plymouth Laira right up to the demise of the GWR. Their retention here for so long was their usefulness in piloting duties over the steep South Devon inclines.

The 10.30 from Plymouth was due to be formed brake third, 'Dining Car unit', composite, third, brake third. These were all 70ft stock, except for the dining car unit, which here appears to have been a two car set. However, on this occasion, a 70ft luggage or newspaper brake van and a 70ft 'Toplight' have been added to the front and there is at least one additional coach on the rear. On reaching Newton Abbot, two more thirds plus a 70ft brake third and a 70ft composite were due to be added. So from there, No. 6001 would have its work cut out hauling (at least) twelve or thirteen coaches up to Whiteball summit!

This superb photograph is an enlargement of the front cover picture. I had hoped here to include the image on the glass plate in its entirety, to show the full extent of the scene as captured by Norman. However, this would have resulted in the divide between the two pages occurring across the boiler of the 'King', which would have spoilt the effect.

In looking at this photograph, I am drawn to the thought that perhaps we had become all too accustomed to the limitations of smaller format film stock, certainly until the more recent advent of the digital image. It is only when seeing images like this we can appreciate why just a few stalwarts, such as Norman Lockett, continued to persevere with a bulky and heavy press camera, with the inconvenience of fragile glass plate negatives, when most others had opted to transfer their allegiance to more modern, lightweight photographic equipment. What the digital age has also given us, however, is the ability to reproduce the images 'as they were taken'. It is only when you see them like this that the amount of tone lost in the dark room can be appreciated, usually having been sacrificed on the altar of contrast!

Extract from the GWR General Appendix to the Rule Book (from August 1936):

WORKING OF ENGINES IN STEAM COUPLED TOGETHER

4-6-0 60XX 'King' class engines:

'King' class engines may run coupled to any engine of the tender type except those in the 'red' group, but 2-6-0 engines of the 83XX and 93XX types are specially authorised. Tank engines of the 'yellow' group only may run coupled to a 'King' class engine.

When any tender engine is run coupled to a 'King' engine, they must not be coupled funnel to funnel.

[Note: Certain other restrictions were listed]

Moving forward in time, to around the beginning of 1949, restrictions were relaxed to enable two 'King' Class locomotives to run coupled together. Whether this applied generally or only to defined sections of the main line is a detail about which I am unsure but certainly it applied to the section between Newton Abbot and Plymouth because, in 1950, the summer service provided for such a working. On Saturdays that summer, the 'Cornish Riviera' changed engines at Newton Abbot and the 'King' which brought this service from Paddington then worked to Plymouth piloting the following 10.35am ex-Paddington (itself a 'King' hauled diagram).

It was Bank Holiday Sunday 1939 and large numbers of people were making the most of the many 'extras' to be run; day trips for what would prove to be the last peace-time holiday break for several years. At 9.50am, No. 4932 *Hatherton Hall* and No. 5041 *Tiverton Castle* storm up the 1 in 42 gradient with an excursion from Plymouth to Bristol. *6th August 1939*

BANK HOLIDAY TRAFFIC

A few pages earlier, I made reference to the summer holiday SX service which ran, for four weeks only, from Saltash to Exeter, with carriages removed at Newton Abbot for stations to Paignton. On Saturdays only, during the same summer period, the complete train (but timed to start from Saltash at 10.19am) ran to Paignton, with reversal at Newton Abbot. In addition, during the Monday to Friday of the August Bank Holiday week only, the Paignton portion off the Exeter service also ran as a separate daily excursion, leaving Saltash at 9.46am. In every case, these trains called only at the stations and halts between Saltash and North Road before a non-stop run to Newton Abbot. On August Bank Holiday (then always the first Monday of the month), Norman Lockett photographed the 9.46am Saltash-Paignton climbing vigorously towards Hemerdon summit. Laira based No. 5041 *Tiverton Castle* was in use again, on this occasion assisted by 'Mogul' No. 8350. The train consists of another very mixed bag of coaches, the second a 'Concertina', so called because all the doors were recessed slightly into the body. *7th August 1939*

AUTO TRAIN SERVICES

The 10.35am (Sundays Only) Plymouth Millbay-Tavistock railmotor (the leading trailer is No. 72) pauses at Mutley station and appears to have some custom. Doubtless this includes those setting off for a day or half-day in the picturesque countryside traversed by much of the Launceston Branch. Mutley station, through which also passed the Southern Railway services to and from the terminus at Friary, was destined to remain open just a further eleven months, a victim of the close proximity of North Road station and of the growth in local bus services. *3rd April 1938*

The service seen here was a typical Plymouth suburban motor train, comprising an 0-6-0PT and a pair of 70ft auto trailers. The 10.35am (SuO) Millbay-Tavistock was to be formed of an auto engine and two trailers until 1st May, from which date a Plymouth Division 'E set' (brake composite, lavatory third, brake third) took over. Instructions were given that, on 'fine Sundays', the trains were to be made up to a full engine load – presumably in anticipation of greater patronage!

The majority of the auto workings westwards from Plymouth ran only as far as Saltash but provided an essential service when, prior to the opening of the Tamar Road Bridge in 1961, the railway and the ferry were the only local means of crossing direct to and from Plymouth. However, some of these motor services extended a little farther west, to St. Germans or Menheniot or, as here, to Liskeard. With the 0-6-0PT sandwiched between two pairs of railmotor coaches, the 5.50pm (SX) from North Road passes Trerule Foot en route to Liskeard, where arrival was scheduled at 6.32pm. *15th August 1939*

This train spent most of the day shuttling between Plymouth Millbay and Saltash, although it did visit St. Germans in the morning. In the afternoon it travelled out to Tavistock and back, followed by this trip to Liskeard. The final journey of the day was a late night return working to Tavistock. It is comprised of an auto fitted 0-6-0PT (here working bunker-first) sandwiched between two pairs of trailers, another common formation in the Plymouth area.

APPROACHING TRERULE FOOT

ABOVE: No. **4953** *Pitchford Hall* nears the end of the long climb from Lynher Viaduct, east of St. Germans, with the 10.35am Wolverhampton to Penzance. The location is the last overbridge westwards before reaching Trerule Foot. The train was due into Liskeard, another 3½ miles, at 5.35pm, so must have been running right time as Norman recorded the time here as 5.30pm. The locomotive had transferred to Penzance just a few years earlier, in January 1935, but was reallocated to Truro in April that same year and remained there until transferred to Pontypool Road in May 1941. *1st August 1939*

No. 4953 was withdrawn in May 1963 and acquired by Woodhams, of Barry, in November 1963. Purchased by the Dean Forest Railway in 1984 and restored at Tyseley Locomotive Works, the locomotive returned to steam in February 2004. No. 4953 has seen much use since on the Sunday Birmingham-Stratford-on-Avon 'Shakespeare Express' services, in addition to other main line workings and guest appearances at various heritage railways.

Norman recorded this train as a Liverpool-West of England service and the time as 6.45pm. He was correct insofar as the stock seen here originated from Liverpool (except one from across the Mersey at Birkenhead) and also that, other than the rear coach, bound for Newquay, all were destined for Penzance. However, earlier in the journey seven coaches had been dropped off – two from Manchester for Cardiff, four from Manchester for Kingswear and one from Liverpool for Kingswear. The Birkenhead coach had been added at Shrewsbury, whilst the Liverpool and Manchester coaches had come together at Crewe to form this train, the 10.32am (SX) Crewe to Penzance service. Further, on this occasion the stock appears to have been marshalled to include an extra LM&SR coach. The 'booked' formation was of GWR stock, excepting that, on alternate days, the dining car was provided by the LM&SR. This, however, was obviously one of the days when the diner (the penultimate coach seen above, although it should have been positioned two from the rear!), was a GWR vehicle. No. 6861 *Crynant Grange* was more than ten minutes down on the scheduled time and, although far from evident when judged by the grubby external condition, the locomotive – allocated to Bristol, St. Philip's Marsh – had been released new to service just 5½ months earlier. *1st August 1939*
The location at and approaching Trerule Foot, as featured on these and some earlier pages, is one we cannot recall as having been illustrated in previous railway books. Perhaps it was just overlooked by other photographers? As far as we have been able to ascertain, we think these pictures represent what turned out to be Norman's last ever visits here.

OPPOSITE PAGE BOTTOM: Another case where the exact location was confirmed by a lineside milepost! Churchward 'Mogul' No. 8357 climbs westwards with a Class 'H' freight, whilst the fireman takes the opportunity for a breather between his exertions on this very exposed section of line. To see just how exposed, have a look at the picture on the rear cover of this book, taken at the same location. The tree on the right in that photograph leaves no doubt as to the direction of the prevailing winds! *15th August 1939*
This locomotive was another of the class which was modified to minimise flange wear by inserting a heavy casting behind the buffer plank. The engine had carried the number 5357 until it was modified and to which number it reverted when put back to its original condition in January 1945. Also clearly visible here is the ATC shoe, the installation of Automatic Train Control having been completed between Plymouth and Penzance only a few years earlier.

The evening sunlight is at its best for photography here as No. 5094 *Tretower Castle* sweeps past with the 1.40pm Paddington-Penzance express. Another member of the class makes a more sedate passage eastwards, returning light engine towards Plymouth. *1st August 1939*

No. 5094, barely six weeks old and allocated to Newton Abbot when seen here, was the second member of the class to carry the name in two years. Tretower Castle had been allocated to No. 5064 when new in June 1937 but that was one of the batch which, later the same year, was renamed by the GWR as 'Earls' (see page 69). Incidentally, I suspect Norman would have been rather annoyed by the sudden appearance of the light engine, which is possibly why he never made a print from the glass plate. I, however, was delighted when David came up with this negative because, there, on the extreme right, is the roadway which enabled me to confirm exactly the whereabouts of the location.

TRERULE FOOT

Trerule Foot (two words and apparently pronounced as 'Troole Foot') is how Norman spelled this hamlet, and how the Ordnance Survey showed it on their maps at least until the early 1960s, but which, nowadays, appears to be preferred in the style of a single word – Trerulefoot. This may stem from the building of a large roundabout on the A38 trunk road, where it meets the A374, with adjacent café and petrol station, which today appears to be the village's main landmark and claim to fame!

Norman takes advantage of the newly opened Trerule Signal Box to capture this image of Laira's No. 4093 *Dunster Castle* **in charge of the 5.15pm stopping train from Plymouth, North Road to Truro.** *15th August 1939*

A signal box was first opened hereabouts around 1907 and closed circa 1927, having been shown as temporarily closed in the 1926 WTT. I am reliably informed that it was purchased by one of the locals at Trerule and used as a garden shed! Trerule box (new) was ordered on 2nd February 1938 and divided the long section between St. Germans and Menheniot. However, it was also sited here because this was to be the junction of a newly announced branch line to Looe, for which purpose provision was made with a lever frame much larger than required merely to serve as a 'break section' box. The scheme was to be financed by Government money as part of the nationwide attempt to alleviate the high unemployment of the 1930s. Although it failed to materialise, the contract for one section was let and some preparatory earthworks as well as at least one overbridge were constructed, before the project was deferred because of the war and never resurfaced. It would have provided a much improved service to the seaside town and avoided a change of train at Liskeard and the reversal at Combe Junction on the existing Looe Branch line, although the construction involved would have been immense, including three tunnels, one of which would have been nearly a mile long, and two large masonry viaducts.

Trerule Signal Box had an interior staircase, so it is almost certain that Norman Lockett was standing on the brick wall of the coal bunker to obtain his photograph. There are many little details of incidental interest in this photograph for the modeller, from the roses grown by the local linesmen in front of their hut on the Up side of the line, to the stack of salt-glazed drainage pipes and the Council roadmen's covered trailer on the extreme right. The Trerule Down Home signal with its tubular post was, of course, a new fixture here and, I suspect, was the reason why he appears never to have made a print of this picture! However, I included this scene because of all the incidental little items of interest. How I wish, though, that Norman had walked back up the lineside a few yards and turned his camera in the opposite direction to photograph an Up train and, by so doing, captured for posterity an image of the new signal box. Perhaps it was the western setting sun that dissuaded him!

'PERFECT SEQUENCE!'

The photographs shown on this and the page opposite have both been published previously – but never next to each other. The significance of placing them together is that although they were taken consecutively (NL negative No's 528 & 529), the respective dates are nearly seven years apart! The reason? The Second World War. As David has commented previously when looking out the two glass plates, *"Perfect sequence, no explanation provided* [in his father's notes] – *perhaps a reflection of the 'British Bulldog' spirit!"*

A little more than two weeks separate this photograph and the start of the Second World War. It proved to be Norman's last opportunity to make a lineside visit in pursuit of his hobby and I doubt whether, on that Tuesday evening spent at Trerule, he could have imagined that nearly seven years would elapse before circumstances enabled him to take his next railway photograph. It was, perhaps, somewhat appropriate that the locomotive here was No. 5071 *Clifford Castle* (then only fourteen months in service from new and based at Newton Abbot), because it was in honour of the brave endeavours played out in the skies during the coming war that led to the renaming of a group of the 'Castle' Class to commemorate famous aircraft associated with the Battle of Britain. No. 5071 was the first, in early September 1940, and carried perhaps the most memorable of these new names – *Spitfire*. The train, by the way, was the 1.40pm Paddington to Penzance. *15th August 1939*
Coincidentally, there is almost a complete history of GWR main line carriages (1904-1939) forming this train, although not in date order! The first and fifth coaches appear to be Collett 'South Wales' type brake thirds of 1922-3, with the luggage compartments leading and trailing respectively, as they should. The second coach is a 'Concertina' third of 1906-7, the third a 'Toplight' composite (1907-21), the fourth a 'Dreadnought' diner of 1904-5, and the final coach a nearly new Collett deep window brake composite, bound for Newquay.

SECTION 3
POST-WAR AUSTERITY (BUT PLENTY OF VARIETY)

More than a year after VE (Victory in Europe) Day, and nine months after the end of the Second World War, Norman Lockett was able, at last, to make some time available for his lineside hobby. Having been instructed by his employer, Boots the Chemist, to manage a variety of stores all around the country during the war years, in 1946 Norman was appointed to take over the management of the Boots branch in Southmead, Bristol. This enabled him to return to live with his family who, during 1940, had moved from Plymouth to Weston-super-Mare, his 'home town'.

However, these were still years of austerity as, slowly, the country started a long haul to rebuild its industrial, commercial and residential base from the horrors of the war. For Norman, like most employees, it was still a five-and-a-half day working week, each day – including travelling time – involving at least twelve hours away from home (plus one late finish when on duty chemist rota). So, for the most part, his photographic forays were still limited to Sundays, Wednesday afternoons and, during the summer months, perhaps an evening spent at the lineside somewhere near his home. Even

so, over the next few years, Norman amassed a sizeable number of photographs, as has become very evident with David having scanned the glass plate negative of every photograph taken by his father, in the vicinity of Weston, during the few years between the end of the war and the demise of the GWR. Even after putting a lot of these to one side, we were still left with a substantial choice, so much so that we questioned with our publisher whether we really should include so many which feature repeatedly the same (or adjacent) lineside locations. In the end, we all agreed 'yes', because this provides a wonderful collage of what, until the start of the 1960s, all railway enthusiasts took so much for granted – the simple pleasure of turning up at the lineside at any time of day, perhaps for no more than an hour, to photograph, 'spot', or merely to watch the passing cavalcade of motive power and traffic. These photographs also provide an insight to a few miles of the GWR system which, to the best of our knowledge, most (if not all!) of Norman's contemporaries elected to ignore. As such, these illustrations will prove a valuable record of the lines which crossed the moors and levels of this part of Somerset.

After a break of six years and ten months, this is Norman's first post-war photograph, taken just south of Brean Road Halt, between Weston-super-Mare and Highbridge. On a sunny summer evening, Class '28XX' 2-8-0 No. 2828, a long-term resident of Aberdare shed, trundles across the Levels with a lengthy westbound Class 'H' freight. *12th June 1946*
Sights such as this must have seemed a million miles removed from what had been endured during the war years – nothing in this view has apparently changed since pre-war days except, perhaps, the external cleanliness of the 2-8-0. However, just half an hour up the line, in Bristol, the ravages of the war-time air raids, as suffered by so many major towns and cities, were all too evident. Nearer to hand, Weston had been bombed on several occasions, with the heaviest air raids during 1941 and '42. It would take until the early years of the 1950s before life returned fully to 'normal' and many more before most of the physical scars of the war were finally removed.

The 5.55pm Wellington to West Ealing milk train is hurried northwards by Bristol, St. Philip's Marsh-based No. 6850 *Cleeve Grange*. Notice the short train consists of rail and road mounted milk tankers together with a van which, in addition to the guard, generally conveyed any churns or tinned milk traffic. Brent Knoll is again prominent in the left distance. *19th June 1946*

Turning around to look north again, and just five minutes after taking the photograph opposite, another Bristol-based locomotive (although one of Bath Road's allocation this time) is featured. No. 5096 *Bridgwater Castle* is in charge of the early evening 'stopper', the 5.50pm Bristol-Taunton, south of Brean Road Halt and heading towards the town whose name it carried. Calling first at Yatton, it was then a case of 'all stations and halts' to Taunton but pausing at Brean Road to set down only on notice being given to the guard at Weston-super-Mare! Norman noted the time as 6.55pm, about 3 minutes down on schedule, so perhaps a request stop had just been made on this occasion. *19th June 1946*

'DOWN BRANCH' TO WESTON

The driver of No. 5018 *St Mawes Castle* casts an eye towards David Lockett's elder brother Geoff, who watches from the public footpath which crossed the Weston 'loop line' beside the Up Branch Distant signal for Worle Junction. The train is the 12.05pm (Sundays) Crewe-Plymouth. No. 5018 was, at the time, based at Wolverhampton (Stafford Road), having returned from an intermediate overhaul at Swindon just a few days earlier. Hence the locomotive (but not the tender!) is looking very clean during a period of post-war austerity, when labour was not yet available (nor was affordable) in numbers sufficient to regain the standards of cleanliness which more often prevailed in the era when Norman Lockett had commenced his photography. *23rd June 1946*

Looking rather travel-stained, 'Star' Class No. 4056 *Princess Margaret* prepares to call at Weston Milton Halt with the 7.40pm local service from Bristol to Taunton. *24th June 1946*

How many enthusiasts of that era might have imagined that No. 4056, new in July 1914, would still be seen running on the Western Region of BR a decade after being photographed here by Norman? Very few I would wager. In fact, in the mid-1950s, Bath Road shed was still putting this locomotive out on express train diagrams. Princess Margaret *would prove to be the last of this famous class to remain in service, being officially withdrawn on 28th October 1957 and cut up at Swindon the week ending 23rd November that same year.*

Norman is back at one of his favourite locations on the main line to the south-west of Worle Junction. On this occasion, he appears to have overlooked the need to record the details of the 'Mogul' in charge of this westbound Class 'H' goods train. The rear of an Up freight can be seen heading towards Bristol in the distance. *26th June 1946*

David recalls that this was one of his father's regular choice of locations, which lay within a twenty minute walk of his home – especially convenient for evening visits. The public footpath hereabouts crossed both the main line and the Weston loop just a short distance away. Therefore, with his good knowledge of rail traffic, Norman was able to move to and fro between the two routes. Some evenings during the late 1940s, Norman might arrange for his eldest son, Geoff, to carry his father's camera and glass plate negatives to Weston Milton Halt and meet him off the train when returning from work in Bristol. "I, being that much younger", recalls David, "was never so entrusted!"

'DOWN MAIN' TO UPHILL

At Sunday mid-day, 'Mogul' No. 9318 heads along the main line towards Hutton with a Down Class 'H' train of empty wagons. In 1940, a new signal box was opened at Hutton, about mid-way between Worle and Uphill junctions. This box had been provided to control a crossover and sidings serving a factory set up that year (a shadow factory to Filton, Bristol) by the Bristol Aeroplane Company for the production of the famous Bristol Beaufighter aircraft. Hutton Signal Box – generally working a single turn on weekdays only – was closed in early June 1964. *14th July 1946*
The '93XX' series was the final development of the extremely useful '43XX' Class first introduced by Churchward in 1911. Built during Collett's regime at Swindon, the '93XX' locomotives were effectively an updated version of this mixed traffic class. Dating from 1932, the final series, like the modified engines which became the '73XX' series, carried a heavy casting fixed behind the front buffer beam which restricted their use to 'red' routes under the GWR system of classification for routing purposes. They too were later modified by the removal of this feature (during the latter half of the 1950s), the reduction of their weight enabling them to be reclassified, as 'blue' route engines, whereupon they were renumbered into the '73XX' series.

OPPOSITE PAGE TOP: The driver acknowledges Norman with a wave of his cap as No. 5065 *Newport Castle* heads away from Weston-super-Mare and nears Worle Junction with the 7.00am (Sundays) Plymouth-Paddington. The locomotive was based at Old Oak and was beginning the run back towards its home shed where, other than visits to Works at Swindon, it remained based until withdrawn in early January 1963. *7th July 1946*
Originally, the nameplates Newport Castle *had been carried by No. 5058 between May 1937 (when new) to September 1937, when it was renamed* Earl of Clancarty. *The* Newport Castle *plates were thereupon transferred to No. 5065 which, only two months earlier, had entered service carrying the name* Upton Castle. *The latter name was, in turn, reallocated to No. 5093 when completed at Swindon in June 1939!*

OPPOSITE PAGE BOTTOM: No wave this time – merely a glance from the driver of 'Castle' No. 5076 *Gladiator* in charge of the 10.40am (Sundays) Liverpool-Plymouth. Weston Milton Halt, the Down platform of which is visible, stands just to the rear of the train. *8th September 1946*
Built in 1938, No. 5076 was named Drysllwyn Castle *and was another of the batch renamed by the GWR and given the names of aircraft following the Battle of Britain. No. 5076 received the new name in January 1941, the original nameplates being re-used on No. 7018 when new into traffic in May 1949. At the time of Norman's photograph, No. 5076 was based at Bath Road.*

WHAT'S IN A NAME? – 2

'THE DEVONIAN' (IN ALL BUT NAME!)

Norman referred, in his notes to the trains featured on this page and opposite as being 'The Devonian', a pre-war service linking Bradford and Paignton. To be more accurate, on most days it had comprised three through coaches which were transferred at Bristol to other services operated by the GWR and LM&SR. However, this 'named' through train had been withdrawn (in both directions) with the introduction of the *Emergency Time Table* immediately following the outbreak of the Second World War. The title was not officially reinstated until the start of the *Summer Time Table* in 1949. With the gradual revival of services following the war years, I suspect, by the autumn of 1946, the train had been restored in all but name, with timings the same, or very similar, to those as used for the pre-war titled service. Possibly, therefore, railwaymen, some regular users and enthusiasts alike referred to the untitled train by its former name. Certainly, as seen here, full sets of coaches (seemingly GWR and LM&SR alternating) could now be observed working through in both directions, although this may not yet have become a regular occurrence.

Having called at Weston-super-Mare, yet-to-be-named 'County' Class No. 1001 heads the service which, in 1949, would become the northbound 'Devonian' east of Weston Milton Halt, on the approach to Worle Junction. Allocated to Newton Abbot, No. 1001 would work the train through to Bristol Temple Meads. The train here extends to nine coaches, all of which appear to be in (clean!) brown & cream GWR livery. *23rd September 1946*
Frederick Hawksworth's 2-cylinder 'County' Class was introduced in 1945. No. 1001, the second to be released into traffic, just twelve months prior to when photographed here, had been allocated the name County of Bucks *but did not receive nameplates until December 1947. Unlike No. 1000, which entered traffic with a double blastpipe and chimney, No. 1001 was built with a single blastpipe and chimney, and this became the standard for all other members of the class until, between 1956-9, all were fitted with a different design of double chimney. So here, in effect, we have a locomotive yet to receive its nameplates heading a service yet to regain its name!*

Norman recorded this photograph, timed at 4.40pm, as featuring what he referred to as the westbound 'Devonian' (the 10.25am Bradford to Kingswear), running about 10 minutes behind schedule west of Worle Junction prior to calling at Weston-super-Mare station. No. 4954 *Plaish Hall* pilots 'Castle' class No. 5079 *Lysander*, heading what was a full LM&SR set of coaches, the leading locomotive attached, possibly, to avoid a light engine working. *23rd September 1946*
Originally named as Lydford Castle, No. 5079 received the new name Lysander in November 1940.

NEAR WORLE JUNCTION: FREIGHT...

'Mogul' No. 7308, with a train of empties returning westwards, is seen from the Down side of the main line. This locomotive was unusual in being one of a batch of fifteen of these 2-6-0s built at Swindon but using parts supplied by Robert Stephenson & Co. *23rd September 1946*

Heavily work-stained 'Grange' Class 4-6-0 No. 6826 *Nannerth Grange* passes by with another lengthy westbound freight, on a sunny late-morning during the final autumn of the GWR. *1st October 1947*

...AND PASSENGER

Looking north-east along the main line towards Worle Junction, No. 6901 *Arley Hall* is in charge of a late-afternoon westbound parcels train, watched by a young David Lockett, left. The second vehicle is an ex-L&NWR passenger brake van, the two-colour look possibly a trick of the light. *15th September 1946*

The lightly loaded 5.50pm (Sundays) Bristol Temple Meads to Weston-super-Mare service poses no problem for No. 6876 *Kingsland Grange*, a long-time allocation to Bristol, St. Philip's Marsh shed. The train is about to pass the 135¾ milepost between Worle Junction and Weston Milton Halt. *7th July 1946*

THE OIL-FIRING EXPERIMENT

The oil-firing experiment of 1945-8 has puzzled many railway historians. Early in 1947, the United Kingdom faced bankruptcy. The imbalance between imports over exports forced the government to accept an American loan, with crippling conditions attached. Yet, despite this overpowering trade deficit and a regime of financial dependency, the government was prepared to import oil to replace an indigenous fuel and use it to power a sizeable proportion of the country's steam locomotive fleet. Why?

Despite there being plentiful supplies of coal underground, overall there was a serious lack of all types of fuel in the two years after the war, with labour having to be drafted into the coal mines in large numbers. Optimistic (but what soon proved to be very unrealistic) data about the coal which could be provided created a post-war crisis, with the Government only realizing the gravity of the fuel supply problem when it was too late to prevent the introduction of electricity blackouts. The GWR Company, only too aware of the situation and the rising cost of coal, had already taken a unilateral decision in 1945 to experiment with oil fuelling and by the end of July 1946 had converted eleven of its '28XX' Class locomotives, plus one 'Hall' Class.

To add to the nation's woes, the winter months of early 1947 were to prove the coldest in living memory. Power cuts had to be introduced, domestic coal was effectively rationed and train services reduced or withdrawn.

Faced with these ongoing problems, at the end of July 1946 the Government effectively ordered the railways to convert a further 1,217 steam locomotives to oil-firing. Just less than 100 had been converted, when not only did it become evident that supply problems were much delaying the scheme, but doubts were raised that there would be sufficient monies available from the Government to complete and maintain the programme! However, by that date, more than £2 million had been expended across the country, not least on oil storage facilities at various locomotive depots, chosen to be a part of what many considered turned out to be a costly fiasco. The entire scheme was abandoned in May 1948, the GWR – perhaps – having led the field with the conversion programme and associated works.

(With acknowledgement to the detailed article 'Oil for Coal' by A.J. Mullay, Railway Archive *Issue 12, Lightmoor Press, March 2006)*

No. 4855, converted to oil burning and renumbered (previously 3813), heads down the main line between Worle and Uphill junctions with a heavy westbound freight. *6th March 1948*
Just a little ahead of the period depicted in other views on the adjacent pages and a photograph which has appeared before but never to a format which does it such justice as here. An evocative scene which, David Lockett is sure, his father would have 'composed' deliberately to include that pair of pollarded willows so typical of the moors and wetlands of much of this part of Somerset. The driver appears very relaxed as a lazy trail of exhaust drifts across the landscape; did it, I wonder, impart a 'fragrance' of burnt oil!

BACK ON BLEADON LEVEL

Class '73XX' 2-6-0 No. 7316 hurries an Up local train northwards having last called at Brent Knoll, the station about 1½ miles to the south. Norman noted this as the 5.08pm Taunton (ex-3.40pm from Exeter) to Bristol Temple Meads but – if so – the time he recorded taking the photograph would have meant the train was running 30 minutes late. Perhaps, therefore, this was the following 5.40pm Taunton to Weston-super-Mare stopper, which was scheduled to pass this spot at the very time recorded by Norman. *7th August 1946*
David is not so sure! His father, he reminded me, studied the local timetables at great length and only very rarely confused the subjects of his photographs. When he was unsure of such details he generally made no reference to a specific service. The signal seen in the background of Norman's photograph was the Up Distant for Lympsham, which was effectively a 'break section' box between Uphill Junction and Brent Knoll that generally opened during the daytime (one shift only) from Mondays to Saturdays. It was taken out of use in December 1958.

Bristol, Bath Road-based No. 4954 *Plaish Hall* **lays a smoke trail whilst accelerating a Down parcels train across Bleadon Level. Here, a minor road runs southwards and parallel with the Up side of the railway for nearly a mile. Doubtless this provided Norman with easy access to the lineside. Nowadays, access hereabouts is barred to all by a tall metal palisade security fence.** *27th September 1946*

Another of the once-numerous mixed traffic 'Moguls', No. 9316, trundles southwards towards Lympsham Signal Box with a Class 'H' freight, possibly a Stoke Gifford to Tavistock Junctior working. The lengths of rail and new sleepers have been off-loaded here ready for some relaying works. The higher ground – Bleadon Hill – acting as the right backdrop to this and similar views forms, in effect, the western extremity of the Mendips, which extend eastwards for many miles across Somerset to reach beyond Shepton Mallet. *27th September 1946*

The weather conditions here (and opposite page, bottom) must have presented Norman with a dilemma – the late afternoon sun is well into the west (to the left here, as witness the shadows). The blustery wind, however, is from the south-sou' east! Norman remained on the Down side of the line and put up with the exhaust blowing across the near-side of the train. I think the result is rather atmospheric – but being one who strived for perfection, I doubt whether Norman ever made a print of this shot!

THE CLIMB TOWARDS WHITEBALL TUNNEL

Norman took a liking to this spot on Wellington Bank, which is just to the south of Beam Bridge where the line passed over the A38 road, about 2 miles south-west of Wellington station. Hereabouts, the gradient hardened to 1 in 80 on the challenging climb towards Whiteball Tunnel and the summit just beyond. On a sunny Wednesday afternoon, No. 6002 *King William IV* storms up the incline in charge of the 1.30pm Paddington-Penzance express. According to the time recorded by Norman (4.50pm), the train was about 5 minutes down on schedule, but with 4 minutes recovery time allowed to Exeter, a 'right time' arrival there was all but assured. *10th July 1946*

My reference, above, to the railway passing over the A38 here is, of course, no longer relevant. Since 1963, the contrary has been the case, the main road – now on a different alignment and widened – bridging the railway. From late 1976, most of the traffic which had formerly used this once busy section of the route to the West Country has been carried on the M5 motorway. Back in 1946, Norman travelled by train to Taunton or Wellington, then caught a bus which would have brought him to Beam Bridge.

The signal arm just visible above the train in this and other photographs featuring this location was the Down Home IBS (intermediate block signal), which served to divide the 3¾ mile section between the signal boxes at Wellington and Whiteball Siding, and over which the scheduled running time for an unfitted Down freight was around 17 minutes.

NEAR YATE

A rare venture to a lineside north of Bristol. 'Near Yate' was Norman's rather vague description, so this being a Down train, the location has to be the spur diverging from the former Midland Railway at Yate South Junction towards (what was at that time) Westerleigh North Junction and, beyond, the junctions with the GWR London to South Wales (and Bristol) main line. No. 3808 climbs around the curve with a Class 'F' freight heading southwards towards Bristol. This connecting line was, until more recent times, a single track, as the corresponding Up line had diverged to cross over the Midland route before joining the same at Yate South Junction. *5th August 1946*

The Midland route is hidden in Norman's view, running in a cutting between the two fence lines seen between the front of the 2-8-0 and the tree to the left. The mileage post records the distance from Paddington, via the Badminton direct line and the east to north chord at Westerleigh. This chord had been opened in the early years of the 1900s, closed in 1927, re-opened as a war-time connection in 1942 and was finally taken out of use again in January 1950. No. 3808 survived in service until withdrawn from Newport during the w/e 10th July 1965. The locomotive was sold (from storage at Cardiff East Dock) to scrap merchants Birds of Morrison on 25th August 1965.

BELOW: I doubt whether Norman would have ever made a print from his negative of this photograph for the obvious reason – the existence of that telegraph pole! It was taken at 8.15pm, as confirmed by the clock on the front of the running shed. To me, however, it's a poignant reminder of the view from the western end of what was then platform 4 at Bristol Temple Meads; when it was possible to sit on a 4-wheeled luggage trolley and watch the numerous light engine workings on and off Bath Road motive power depot. Still coded 'BRD' at the time of this view but '82A' by the time when, occasionally, I used to come here in the 1950s, this is the classic view of the locomotive shed and depot, set against a backcloth of the terraced houses in the Totterdown and Knowle districts of the city. *26th May 1947*

RIGHT: Norman Lockett was always very proud of his 'home' county and anything associated with it, so the nameplate attached to No. 4016 was an obvious candidate to be recorded whilst he was waiting at Temple Meads station for his train home to Weston-super-Mare. Built as a 'Star' Class in 1908, No. 4016 originally carried the name *Knight of the Golden Fleece* and this was retained when the locomotive was rebuilt as a 'Castle' in 1925. The renaming as *The Somerset Light Infantry (Prince Albert's)* was undertaken in January 1938. Notice this is a special one-piece nameplate, with no separate distance piece between the splasher and plate. Pictured here whilst paused in front of the Locomotive Yard Signal Box, No. 4016 was withdrawn from Old Oak Common shed on 24th September 1951. *17th May 1948*

A 'one-off' visit by Norman (at least prior to 1950); this is the main line near Pilning, east of the Severn Tunnel. 'Castle' Class No. 5085 *Evesham Abbey* (based at Old Oak Common), with a South Wales-Paddington express, climbs the 1 in 100 gradient which, apart from a ½ mile of level track between Pilning station and Junction, continues all the way from the bottom level in the tunnel to Patchway, a distance of more than 4½ miles. No. 5085 was, in effect, a re-build in 1939 from 'Star' Class No. 4065, which had carried the same name. This appears to be a train originating in West Wales, with the coaches at the front, including the dining car (the second coach), added at Swansea. *26th May 1947*

The tunnel mouth seen in the background is Ableton Lane Tunnel (97 yards long). The entrance to the Severn Tunnel lies about a ¼ mile farther west. Note the goods loops on either side of the main running lines; the Down loop with the intermediate exit and complete with locomotive watering facility – the lineside column supplied from the storage tank seen towards the top of the cutting. The notice board (the rear of which is seen bottom right) by the side of the Up Main line is a warning of 'Spring Points' ahead – a set of spring-action trailing points which led to a sand drag; essential to divert any 'runaways' which happened to break away from an ascending loose coupled freight train on this long gradient. There were several such sets of points and sand drags between the tunnel mouth and Pilning, over which section freight trains were invariably assisted at the front rather than from behind, which was the practice east of Pilning. Norman probably never bothered to return here as this scene was marred by a very prominent wire and support cable which extended diagonally across the foreground to the signal seen bottom right. I must own up to the fact that, with the agreement of David, I have 'digitally removed' the wire and support cable; an action which, I hope, will not offend the purists amongst you too much!

SECTION 4
FROM GWR TO BR(WR)

As mentioned in the Introduction, David and I decided to end this book with some of Norman's pictures taken during the first two years of the Nationalised era, rather than to conclude at the demise of the GWR. The following pages show, apart from the excitement of the 'locomotive exchanges', how, outwardly at least, little appeared to change during those earliest years of British Railways. There was, of course, the inevitable experimenting with liveries, until such time as some firm decisions were made. Unlike the motive power included in the other regions created by Nationalisation, however, the former GWR numbering remained the same, although the painted numerals on the buffer plank and the shedcode painted on the framing were both replaced by BR with plates affixed to the smokebox door. Note how few examples of these changes Norman photographed though – not deliberately but because such changes were, initially, somewhat few and far between!

A rare visit to Swindon in 1947 enabled Norman to spend an hour at the lineside at the Stratton Road bridge, on the eastern side of the town. No. 4854, built in 1942 (as No. 3837) and here converted to an oil burner, pulls forward with a westbound Class 'H' freight, which is about to be diverted into the Down Goods loop at Highbridge Junction. The oil tank is prominent in the tender of the 2-8-0, which is also fitted with external sliding shutters to the cabside windows. The locomotive ran in this condition until August 1949 when converted back to burn coal, whereupon the original running number was readopted. *27th June 1947*

HIGHWORTH JUNCTION

Norman's notes described the location here only as *'near Swindon'*, so thank goodness for the lineside milepost which reveals the exact spot. This was subsequently confirmed by David, who accompanied his father that day and whose abiding memory was just how far it seemed from Swindon station for a small lad and how frequently he was chided by his father to *"keep up"*!

Thirty-five minutes after taking the photograph opposite, the scene was repeated but this time the 2-8-0, No. 3841 (again of the lot built in early 1942), was not one of the twenty members of this class included in the scheme for conversion to oil burning. The view here appears quite rural but, once beyond the bridge immediately behind Norman's camera position, goods loops were provided on both sides of the two running lines, plus a plethora of sidings controlled, at this end, by Highworth Junction Signal Box. *27th June 1947*

To the casual observer, other than the fitting of outside steam pipes and a modified front end, there was little difference in the appearance of the last of this class, as built during Collett's regime in 1942, to the first of these fine 2-8-0s as designed by Churchward at the beginning of the 20th century. That was, without doubt, a tribute to the soundness of the original design, which sufficed to serve the GWR and the Nationalised successor until the last of the class, No. 3836, was withdrawn w/e 30th October 1965.

Although most of the Swindon railway scene as Norman would have known it has disappeared over time, Highworth Junction has managed to outlast the closure of the Highworth Branch in 1962. Albeit in vastly simplified form and with the signal box having long gone, a short section of the branch continues in freight use, serving the huge Honda car factory and an adjacent scrapyard, Coopers Metals. The latter concern has been trading since the mid 1920s and, on 9th July 1959, purchased for scrapping two ex-GWR '64XX' Class engines, No's 6409 and 6428. The same company also purchased, on 31st December 1964, two of No. 3841's older classmates, No's 2842 and 2872, which were taken to be cut up at their site at Sharpness, Gloucestershire. No. 3841 was withdrawn from Pontypool Road on 10th March 1964 and sold to George Cohen on 23rd April 1964. Most probably the sale was to Cohen's Hereford base (official records vary between here and Kettering), with delivery some time after 3rd May 1964.

ABOVE: Norman had last photographed 'County' Class No. 1001 almost a year previously and here the locomotive is featured again, still yet to acquire its nameplates and this time approaching Worle Junction from the east. The two signals shown are the distants; Up (to the left) for Puxton & Worle and Down for Worle Junction. The train is the 11.55am (SX) Manchester to Plymouth. Departure from Bristol T.M. was scheduled for 6.05pm, passing Worle Junction at 6.27pm and running non-stop to Taunton in one minute over the hour. This train appears to consist entirely of LM&SR (and constituents) stock. The leading coach, and probably the third one, is ex-L&NWR, whilst the second is a Period III Stanier design. Note how reflections from the sky give the coaches a two colour effect. *10th September 1947*
On this side of these locomotives, the position of the reversing rod required the nameplate (when eventually provided!) to be fixed to a metal backplate, whereas on the opposite side, the nameplate was fixed directly to the flat topped splasher. The latter feature, covering all coupled wheels, was a throwback to 1935 when two GWR locomotives were 'semi-streamlined' for a period of time (see pages 26-7). Another unusual feature of this class was the provision of a footstep at the right extremity (left side as viewed here) of the buffer beam.

RIGHT: Laira-based 2-8-0 No. 2857 appears to be 'going well' under a clear back board approaching Worle Junction with a westbound Class 'D' express freight. The fireman looks to be pleased with his efforts – or had he just spotted Norman with his large camera in the field adjoining the lineside? Note the cattle are totally unfazed by all the commotion but, no doubt, they had long become accustomed to sounds of the passing steam hauled traffic. Today, such cattle would find themselves being chased out of the gardens of Verbana Way and Magnolia Avenue, just a small part of the housing developments which now extend all the way east as far as the M5 motorway. I doubt whether Norman would recognise the location all these years later! *5th October 1948*

FOCUS ON FREIGHT

We are deliberately concentrating on freight trains now for the following few pages, all of which will serve as a vivid reminder of just how varied was the goods carried by the railways under the Common Carrier policy until the early 1950s, when road transport began to make much greater inroads (sorry, pun not intended!) into this valuable traffic. This was to prove the final ten years during which the railways were still able to retain much of what had always been their core business. Looking at the length of just this one train, how many road vehicles would be required to shift such a load?

Nearing the end of her years, 'Bulldog' Class 4-4-0 No. 3386 (built in 1903 originally as No. 3448, and withdrawn from Reading on 22nd November 1949) saunters down the main line west of Worle Junction with an evening Class 'J' freight heading towards Highbridge, Bridgwater and Taunton; a far cry from earlier days when, as a top link locomotive, she carried the name *Paddington*. The leading five wagons contain sawn timber (possibly imported via Avonmouth), all securely roped down. *11th July 1947*

As with several others of this class which carried the names of places served by the GWR, the nameplates where removed in May 1927. It has been claimed that this action was taken to avoid possible confusion by passengers with train destinations.

No. 3002 heads westwards at the same location with a Class 'H' freight. I cannot make out what has been chalked onto the side of the tender – perhaps something derogatory as these 2-8-0s were, it has been rumoured, somewhat less than popular with many GWR enginemen! *29th July 1947*

Originally built in large numbers at Gorton for the Ministry of Munitions (for the Railway Operating Division of the Royal Engineers) during 1914-18, a hundred of the many surplus of these 2-8-0s were taken over by the GWR following the First World War. No. 3002 was one of the original batch of twenty purchased by the GWR in 1919, most of which passed into BR ownership twenty-nine years later. However, during 1948 many of these remaining early members of the class were withdrawn (No. 3002 from Pontypool Road on 24th April 1948). Of the one hundred purchased by the GWR, forty-five passed onto BR ownership. By the start of December 1956, only six remained (all then based at Carmarthen), with the last three withdrawn on 17th October 1958. Although re-equipped with many GWR fittings, the class retained their original Great Central Railway type boilers.

Crossing the main line to look westwards, an absolutely immaculate looking oil burning 2-8-0, No. 4808, heads between Hutton and Worle Junction with an Up Class 'E' express freight, possibly a Tavistock Junction-Bristol West Depot service. *24th September 1947*
Plymouth Laira based No. 4808 had only recently (July 1947) been converted to oil burning. Formerly No. 2834 (placed into traffic May 1911) the engine regained its original number in January 1950, the last of the class to be converted back to a coal burner; it was withdrawn from Didcot during the w/e 27th October 1962.

Now looking eastwards again but Norman remained on the 'Down' side of the main line (between Worle and Uphill junctions) to take into account the lighting and prevailing sou-westerly wind. I couldn't resist this one, showing 'the other side' of an ex-ROD Class. Taken at noon on an autumnal Sunday, No. 3005 is plugging away against a strong headwind with a westbound Class 'H' freight. With surplus steam blowing off from the safety valves, the fireman takes 'a breather' from his efforts with the shovel. *26th October 1947*

No. 3005, another of those initial twenty purchased by the GWR in 1919, was withdrawn from service (from Tyseley) on 16th August 1948, less than a year after being seen here by Norman. However, a note in the **Railway Observer** *mentioned the frames of this locomotive were re-used on No. 3033 when at Swindon for repair in autumn 1948.*

Under a clear sky, the impressive sight of hard working 2-8-0 No. 2811, with a lengthy Bristol-bound Class 'J' freight, is sufficient to draw the attention of two young girls at the lineside. It looks as though a picnic may have been temporarily disturbed, as there appears to be a rug laid out on the lower part of the style serving the public footpath which crossed the railway here. The safety valve bonnet on the 2-8-0 appears rather the worse for wear! *11th May 1947*

David recalls there was no doubt that the GWR 2-8-0s were a favourite of his father, a fact that was recounted to me many years ago by Ivo Peters, who frequently attempted to pull Norman's leg by claiming that these Churchward veterans couldn't 'hold a candle' to the pulling and braking power of the S&D 2-8-0s!

This is the type of picture where making a digital scan from a glass plate negative which, (in 2010) is sixty-three years old, is of greatest benefit – just look at the wonderful cloud formation and the exhaust from the 2-8-0, at the head of a westbound Class 'H' freight. The late spring sunshine adds some superb lighting to the scene. The only problem here was that, unusually, Norman forgot to record the locomotive's number! *4th May 1947*

Notice the front raft of wooden-bodied wagons are all sheeted. Instructions regarding the ordering, usage, care and disposal of wagon sheets occupied more than two pages in the GWR General Appendix to the Rule Book issued in 1936.

The same location, but with the wind coming from a different quarter to that featured in the photograph opposite. 'May Day' brings Norman to the lineside to witness ex-Ministry of Supply 'WD' Class 2-8-0 No. 90359 (formerly numbered WD7294, later renumbered 77294) with yet another Class 'H' freight. The vehicle carried in the well wagon (fourth behind the tender) appears to be a military searchlight truck, presumably bound for storage somewhere in the South West. A little farther back there is another well wagon, carrying what we believe to be a threshing machine, which we can speculate may be destined for an agricultural merchant. *1st May 1949*

On pages 117 and 118, we included examples of the 2-8-0s built in large numbers for the War Department during the First World War. Moving forward nearly thirty years, 935 of the Austerity 2-8-0s (as per the example above) were built between 1943 and 1945 for the Ministry of Supply, to the design of R.A. Riddles. The building programme was shared between the North British Locomotive Co. of Glasgow and the Vulcan Foundry of Newton-le-Willows, Lancashire. After the war, 200 were purchased by the L&NER and 533 were divided on loan to the railway companies, with all of them subsequently transferring into BR stock after Nationalisation, to be renumbered into the 90000 series. Allocated to Laira when seen here, No. 90359 was one of the North British engines.

APPROACHING UPHILL JUNCTION

At Uphill Junction, the loop line serving Weston-super-Mare converged to rejoin the original main line from Worle Junction. The loop (or 'branch line', to use the official designation) can just be seen to the left of the lineside hut, on the extreme left of this view. No. 6944 *Fledborough Hall* accelerates a heavy westbound Class 'D' freight along the main line approach to the junction. Built during the war years (in 1942), this locomotive was not provided with nameplates until March 1947 and was allocated to Bristol, St. Philip's Marsh when seen here some nineteen months later. The fireman appears to look suitably relaxed along a section of the main line which, possibly, did not usually overtax one's skill with the shovel! *8th October 1948*

ABOVE: David Lockett, who was with his father at the lineside at the time, recounted this as the only occasion when a driver left his footplate and walked across to Norman to request a copy of a photograph! Norman recorded the fact on the envelope containing the glass plate negative, including the driver's name. So if anyone reading this happens to have known Driver Moore, this is he at the regulator of 'WD' Class 2-8-0 No. 70836 (renumbered 90324 in March 1949). The train is about to draw to a halt to give precedence to a westbound passenger service heading out from Weston-super-Mare station; hence the opportunity for the driver to approach Norman. *31st October 1948*

David recalls that Driver Moore received his photograph from Norman but, unfortunately, the record of the address to which it was sent was not retained. The locomotive was, at the time, allocated to 'SPM' (Bristol, St. Philip's Marsh) before moving to Swindon, then transferring 'up North' to become a long-term resident of Agecroft shed, in Manchester, from where she was withdrawn w/e 2nd May 1964 and sold for scrapping to the Slag Reduction Co. of Rotherham.

At the same location as the previous two photographs, 'Castle' Class No. 5062 *Earl of Shaftesbury* was, according to Norman's note of the time, a few minutes down on schedule, as it hurries past with the 11.25am Cardiff to Kingswear. During this period, No. 5062 was allocated to Newton Abbot shed. As we witnessed earlier, the locomotive was originally named *Tenby Castle*. *9th October 1948*
The line to the right seen here was a goods refuge siding. There appears to be at least one wagon at the far end, possibly used in conjunction with some local track works, or a 'cripple' which had been put off a freight train to await attention. Perhaps it was the source of the fresh stone or sand deposited along the length of the siding; was this deliberate or a leaking wagon?

Moving a hundred yards or so down the line from the previous location, here is the scene just to the south of Uphill Junction which is situated beyond the far side of this overbridge. 'Star' Class No. 4047 *Princess Louise* passes at speed with the 9.10am Manchester (London Road)–Plymouth, a service which, at the time, did not call at Weston-super-Mare. No. 4047 (allocated to Bristol Bath Road shed) will have taken over the train at Temple Meads and remained one of only two of those 'Stars' built in 1914 which was destined never to be fitted with outside steampipes. She was withdrawn, from Bath Road on 30th July 1951 and cut up at Swindon during the four week period ending 8th September that same year. The train consists of both ex-LM&SR and GWR coaches; the first two are LM&SR Period III Stanier designs. *9th October 1948*

This picture is a reminder to David that he and his older brother, Geoff, now sometimes accompanied their father to the lineside, as evidenced here and in other photographs where either one or both might be seen. Both can be seen watching from the roadside to the left of the bridge. David recalls that soon after, they were both old enough to go 'train spotting' without being in the company of their father, a situation which continued for just a few more happy years until training and other matters of life (including National Service) were destined to relegate their interest in railways. Incidentally, David also remarked that "Dad, if making a print, would more than likely have cropped us out!"

SOUTH OF BLEADON & UPHILL

ABOVE: Looking in need of some 'spit & polish', 'Castle' Class No. 5048 *Earl of Devon* heads the 4.15pm (Sundays) Bristol to Plymouth, a service which carried both passenger and parcels traffic. With the post-war economic situation in Britain still dire and the railways to be Nationalised in just four months time, one suspects that engine cleaning was not seen by the GWR as a priority. No. 5048, originally named *Cranbrook Castle*, was another of the class renamed after 'Earls' in 1937 and was at this time based locally at Bath Road. According to the Summer 1947 Bristol Division coach working book, this was a train formed of '*scratch stock – unbalanced*'. As such, it was made up of any suitable stock available in Dr Day's Sidings at Bristol and did not have a train allocated for the return journey. It was supposed to be formed: brake third, two thirds, composite, third, brake third – all corridor coaches. On this day, however, the leading coach was a 'Toplight' brake composite. A van from Nottingham and a passenger brake van from Sheffield, both destined for Penzance, brought up the rear of the train. *31st August 1947*
The bridge shown is the first south of Bleadon & Uphill station (closed 5th October 1964) and carries a local route from the main Bridgwater road (A370) across the railway. It then turns southwards and runs alongside the line for almost a mile (see map on page 128), before re-crossing it by means of the next overbridge.

OPPOSITE PAGE TOP: Looking towards Highbridge, this is about 1½ miles south of the previous view. No. 5047 *Earl of Dartmouth* (formerly *Compton Castle*), running at speed with the 'Northern Mail', passes a westbound train with a 4-wheeled horsebox as tail traffic. The 'Mail' was the 12 noon Penzance to Liverpool which, during this period in time, included a TPO between Plymouth and Bristol. On this occasion, Norman recorded the train running about 6 minutes late and with only 2 minutes recovery time built into the schedule between Worle Junction and Temple Meads, a late arrival there could be anticipated. Luckily 15 minutes were allowed at Bristol for the engine and TPO to be removed, the replacement LMR (*nearly put LM&SR – see below!*) motive power to be attached during which period there would be much unloading and loading of mail traffic. *1st September 1948*
Note the date – eight months into the 'new dawn', the start of the BR era, not that you would realise this by just looking at Norman's photograph. As mentioned earlier, this was one of the reasons why David and I decided to extend the period covered by this book to include 1948-9, because, initially, there was little following Nationalisation which changed outwardly to suggest the GWR had ceased to exist. Even the numbers of the locomotives were destined to stay the same under the new BR numbering system (apparently to avoid having to scrap all the GWR cabside cast numberplates). No. 5047 was based, at the time, at Newton Abbot and was only three months away from a visit to Swindon for a 'heavy general' overhaul.

OPPOSITE PAGE BOTTOM: Turning around from the previous photograph, we now revert to the final year of the GWR. The 6.05pm departure from Bristol Temple Meads was a through Manchester (London Road) to Plymouth train, seen here 'right time' and with No. 6027 *King Richard I* in charge, speeding towards its next scheduled stop at Taunton. The train is formed of LM&SR coaches. *27th May 1947*
Despite the absence of any gradients, it was rumoured that the effects of the strong winds blowing unopposed off the nearby Bristol Channel across this exposed section of the main line could equate to the weight of a couple of additional coaches! David recalls, however, those balmy summer days when it was possible to spend just an hour here in the evening, enabling his father to photograph at least five trains including the 'Milky' and the 'Up Mail'. So this was always a popular trip out after an early tea and, being just a few miles south of Weston, enabled Norman to have his sons back home just before their appointed time for bed.

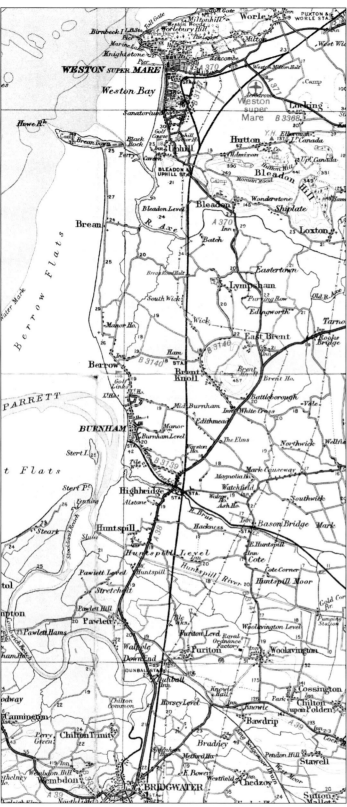

The strength and direction of the prevailing wind are again all too evident as 2-8-0 No. 3833 runs at a sedate speed towards Highbridge with a 'Down' Class 'J' freight. It is evident from the quality of these pictures why Norman so favoured this location for many of his early evening photographic forays, with the sun perfectly positioned for such shots. As he never failed to record, the country was enjoying 'DBST' ('Double British Summer Time'); ideal for the photographer who could only get to the lineside after a day at work. *9th July 1947*

A portion of the Bartholomew's half inch map of North Somerset, which illustrates the almost dead straight section of railway running from Bleadon to Bridgwater. Just south of Bleadon & Uphill station, the railway crosses the River Axe, over which the formation had to be raised to gain sufficient clearance – the only minor 'blip' in this otherwise level stretch of line. Having rounded the curve seen in the photograph on page 126, the railway continues southwards in a dead straight line for mile after mile passing, in turn, Lympsham Signal Box (not shown), Brean Road Halt (closed 1955) and Brent Knoll, before reaching Highbridge, where the S&D line was crossed on the level.

ABOVE: Looking southwards again, the 'Up Milk', the 5.55pm Wellington to West Ealing, hurries by. This had called at Highbridge for 10 minutes, to collect any loaded tankers brought across (via the S&D) from the milk factory at Bason Bridge – not every gallon went out via Templecombe even before the Western Region of BR came into existence! Grimy 'Star' Class No. 4019 *Knight Templar* lays down a trail of exhaust; unusually, the wind is not in the south-west quarter. *27th May 1947*

This locomotive, built in 1908, was still running with inside steam pipes to the cylinders. Outside (elbow pattern) pipes were provided somewhat belatedly exactly twelve months later. Despite this, just a further seventeen months were to elapse before No. 4019 was withdrawn, in October 1949.

RIGHT: The last of the pictures in this book to feature the line across the Levels south of Weston provides this view of another 'Star' turn – No. 4045 *Prince John*, with the early evening local from Taunton to Weston-super-Mare. The signal in the background is the Up Distant for Lympsham box, which normally, by this time of day, will have 'switched out'. A fogman's hut stands adjacent to the signal. The prominent land feature in the left background of both of these views is Brent Knoll, which we referred to on an earlier page. *25th May 1947*

No. 4045, built 1913, was another of the 'Stars' fitted with outside steam pipes very late on in service. The elbow pattern pipes seen here had been provided at the start of 1946 and the locomotive was withdrawn in November 1950.

AROUND WORLE JUNCTION

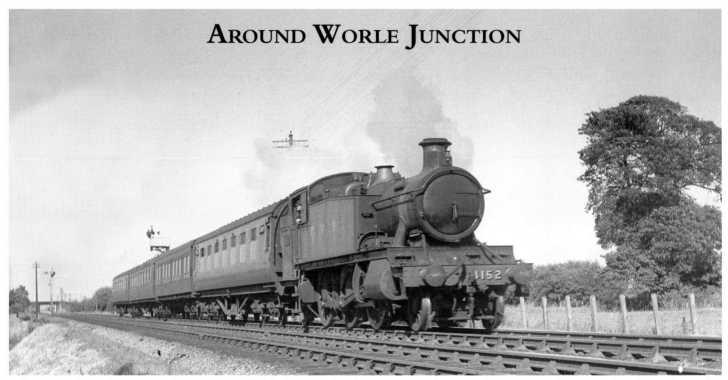

Sunday tea-time finds Norman at the lineside east of Worle Junction, a location he appears to have visited only very occasionally, much preferring favoured haunts half-a-mile or so farther westwards – perhaps because it was that little nearer to his home? 'Large Prairie' No. 4152 is cautioned by the Down Distant for Worle Junction, whilst heading towards the penultimate stop at Weston Milton with the 5.50pm (Sundays) 'stopper' from Temple Meads to Weston-super-Mare, a service which on other days continued through to Taunton. *13th July 1947*
No. 4152 was virtually new, having been placed into service earlier the same year. The locomotive was one of the last batch (No's 4150-59) to be built at Swindon by the GWR, although a final twenty of these popular 'Large Prairies', No's 4160-79, followed during the first two years of Nationalisation. According to the local coach workings book, this train was to be formed of a 'B set' but here we have a four coach train of two LM&SR and two GWR coaches, all corridor stock!

The same location but viewed from the opposite (south) side of the main line and some fifteen months later. Bath Road-based No. 5025 *Chirk Castle* heads the 2.20pm Bristol to Weston-super-Mare local. The leading coach seems to be a 'Concertina' brake third, whilst the second one may still be carrying the wartime all-brown livery. It looks like the signal and the fogman's hut had both recently received the attention of the local painting gang of what, by this date, was the newly formed Western Region of British Railways. You will notice, in contrast to Norman's other shots here, the field to the left of the line is bereft of cattle – perhaps it was afternoon milking time! *5th October 1948*

Providing rather a contrast to the motive power to be found on the following two pages, No. 6004 *King George III* heads towards her home shed in charge of the 5.00pm Paddington-Plymouth express, a heavy train scheduled to contain eight coaches for Plymouth and five for Paignton. The train was due to call at Weston, with arrival timed for 7.53pm. Norman recorded the time here as 8.00pm, so the train was running about 10 minutes late. However with 5 minutes allowed for each of the stops at Weston, Taunton, Exeter, and Newton Abbot, this was not the fastest of 'expresses', so a right time (11.15pm) arrival at Plymouth could almost be guaranteed. *29th July 1947*

TWO ELDERLY LADIES

Norman captured this delightful image west of Worle Junction, with Bath Road shed having turned out elderly 'Dean Goods' 0-6-0 No. 2462, carrying a Class 'G' headcode denoting a Workmans' train. Comprising a couple of ex-LM&SR coaches, the train heads towards Weston Milton in the early evening. Notice the flap under the front of the smokebox, which gave access to some oil cups, had – as was often the case with these veterans – been left open. Dating back to the Victorian era, the locomotive, built as part of Swindon Lot 99 (1895-6), survived until January 1953. *22nd August 1948*

In his book 'GWR Steam' (David & Charles, 1972), O.S. Nock recounts how, right until the post-1948 era, the design of the '2301' Class, which dated back to 1883, influenced new practice, culminating with 'one-off' BR 'Pacific' No. 71000, the twin blastpipe of which matched exactly the dimensions of two 'Dean Goods' blastpipes placed side by side!

Looking very travel weary and destined to be withdrawn just thirteen months hence, 'Bulldog' Class 4-4-0 No. 3376 *River Plym*, in charge of a Class J freight, heads towards Weston. Norman noted the time as 7.55pm, so this could have been the evening (RR) Bristol West Depot-Hackney (Newton Abbot) not running to the scheduled time and 'put around the Weston Loop' at Worle Junction to clear the main line for a following 'runner'. If correct, then in all probability, the latter would have been the 5.05pm Paddington-Plymouth passenger which ran 'main line' between Worle and Uphill junctions. *9th August 1947*
RR: Runs when Required only.

ON THE LOOP

At last, a representative of the 'County' Class complete with nameplates. No. 1028 *County of Warwick*, released into traffic just a month earlier and allocated to 'BRD' (Bristol, Bath Road), with a late running 12.30pm (Sundays) from Paddington, nears its destination at Weston-super-Mare. Notice the straight nameplate, on this side of the locomotive, fixed direct to the flat-topped splasher (*see note to the picture on page 114*). *13th April 1947*
The rear of the train has just passed Weston Milton Halt, situated immediately on the near side of the overbridge (Locking Moor Road) seen in the distance. The halt was much more convenient than the General station at Weston for Norman's daily travels to and from work in Bristol. David recalls that, invariably, his father used the 7.36am departure, with Norman arriving onto the Up platform 'on the dot' and such a regular user that the carriage door would be held open for him – how was that for service!

OPPOSITE PAGE TOP: On a day of bright sunshine and with the Up Branch Distant signal showing 'off', No. 6017 *King Edward IV* gets a clear run from the signalman at Worle Junction with the 7.00am (Sundays) Plymouth-Paddington, another of those winter services which, with a formation including some coaches destined for the north, went the 'Great Way Round' at no great speed, taking nearly 8 hours to reach the capital! *13th April 1947*
The front four coaches of this service were from Taunton, the second four from Plymouth – all bound for Paddington. At the rear were four more coaches from Plymouth to Liverpool, to be detached at Bristol. At Swindon, a van from Calne to Paddington would be attached to the front, doubtless one of those which used to be branded as 'Harris (Calne)' and containing products from the firm's meat processing factory (which has now long ceased to exist) based at the Wiltshire town.

Thought we had better include this one! No. 6024 *King Edward I* hurries across Worle Moor for a 'right time' arrival at Weston-super-Mare with the 5.00pm Paddington-Plymouth. It appears that No. 6024 was a regular performer on this service during the early summer in 1947. *3rd June 1947*
No. 6024 was rescued from Woodham's scrap yard at Barry in 1973 and superbly restored to main line condition by the King (later the 6024) Preservation Society, first running again in full working order in February 1989. During the following twenty years No. 6024 travelled widely across the British main line network, received two further major overhauls, revisited many of its old haunts and celebrated its 75th Anniversary hauling a special from Paddington to Kingswear. In the midst of preparing this book, the writer last saw a resplendent No. 6024 heading a Sunday special along the sea wall at Teignmouth – an event which still draws crowds of onlookers to this famous section of the GWR main line to the West.

ABOVE: Taunton-based 'Prairie' No. 5503 climbs Wellington Bank, passing the 172¾ milepost with the 5.00pm 'stopper'. Evidently, even the more modest GWR service could consist of a variety of coaching stock! Here, the first coach appears to be a steel panelled 'Toplight' brake third, with most of its toplights plated over and apparently still retaining its wartime brown livery, as does the elderly third coach with a clerestory roof. In contrast, the second coach is a relatively modern Collett 'large window' design. *12th May 1948*

A part of the glass plate from which this image has been scanned has acquired a grey cast which, despite efforts to remove with digital imaging software, is still partially evident (see rear two coaches and below). However, this is an interesting photograph – and, in any case, Norman didn't get to photograph a 'Small Prairie' on main line duties too often!

THE '5 O'CLOCK STOPPER'

During late April and May of 1948, Norman made a number of visits back to the lineside on the testing climb towards Wellington Tunnel. The main purpose of these visits is revealed on the following pages but on two successive occasions, he remained at the lineside to photograph the 5.00pm all stations from Taunton to Exeter – the '5 o'clock stopper'.

Six days later, Taunton shed turned out No. 5003 *Lulworth Castle* to provide the motive power for the 5.00pm Down local. On this occasion, there was an LM&SR passenger brake van at the head of the train and the third coach appears to be a GWR 'Dreadnought' brake third (dating from about 1905), with its toplights plated over. *18th May 1948*
This is another location which I had difficulty identifying, as the surroundings to the lineside are now very different (see inset, bottom left, courtesy David Stubbs – the nearest we could achieve without trespassing!). Other than the curvature of the line, the main clue was the crossing (a public footpath just seen in the left background of Norman's shot) where the line curves out of the wooded section. Despite this being a section of track witnessing very high speeds, this foot crossing still survives and is known as Westford, just over half-a-mile south of Wellington station. Norman's view shows the train approaching an overbridge which carries the road from Rockwell Green to Westford.

THE LOCOMOTIVE EXCHANGES: PRE-TEST RUNS

Not long after the Nationalisation of Britain's railways, the newly established Railway Executive announced plans for a series of trials, to ascertain the relative strengths and identify any weaknesses of a range of motive power drawn from the pre-Nationalised companies. This was to be achieved by a series of 'locomotive exchanges', taking place over a period of 4½ months. Amongst the first of the trials scheduled were those on the Paddington-Plymouth route, extending from Monday, 19th April to Friday, 28th May 1948.

The pattern of working agreed was that, for each of the chosen routes, the individual locomotives nominated to take part in the trials for that route would work four pre-test runs (two in both directions) followed by four test runs. Supposedly, the data obtained from the trials was to be taken into account in the designs of the proposed BR 'Standard' classes of locomotives, the first of which would appear three years later, in 1951.

Norman may well have come to the lineside here at Marlands, on the final approach to Whiteball Tunnel, expecting to photograph ex-L&NER Gresley Class 'A4' 'Pacific' No. 60022 *Mallard*. Apparently, however, the famous 'Streak' failed the previous day whilst working the first Up pre-test train from Plymouth to Paddington. So, on what turned out to be a very wet afternoon, No. 60033 *Seagull* was substituted for this, the 1.30pm from Paddington, the service used for the Down pre-test runs and subsequent trial trains. *28th April 1948*
This attractive spot is immediately to the north of the underbridge at Marlands and the cutting which precedes the entrance to the 1,092 yard long Whiteball Tunnel, during the course of which, the railway passes from Somerset into Devon. When visiting this area in 2009, to identify exactly the place from which Norman had taken this and similar photographs, a concrete milepost, replacing that seen in Norman's photograph, confirmed we had found the correct lineside location.

Two weeks later, ex-LM&SR 'Princess Coronation' Class 4-6-2 No. 46236 *City of Bradford*, enjoys much better weather conditions with its second westbound 'pre-test' train on this route. Again the service used for the pre-test was the 1.30pm from Paddington, the locomotive returning the following day with the 8.30am Plymouth-Paddington. *12th May 1948*
Notice the flattened top at the front of the smokebox. Until the end of the previous year, this locomotive had been a 'streamliner' – the removal of the over-cladding revealing how the previously hidden smokebox had been shaped at the top to accommodate the streamlining. It's rather a coincidence that, as this book is being prepared, the preserved 'Princess Coronation', No. 46229 Duchess of Hamilton, has been the subject of a scheme which has resulted in the locomotive reappearing in full streamlined form and attracting much attention after a period of more than sixty years. What a great pity, however, she's not a 'runner'!

ABOVE: In addition to the three 'Pacific' classes used for the Paddington-Plymouth route (LMR 'Princess Coronation', ER 'A4' and SR 'Merchant Navy'), two 4-6-0s were included in the trials – representing the WR 'King' and LMR rebuilt 'Royal Scot' classes. The latter, originally a Fowler design but rebuilt by Stanier, features here in the form of No. 46162 *Queen`s Westminster Rifleman* which, if Norman's timing was correct (and invariably it was), the train was about 6 minutes down on schedule. This was the second of the Down pre-trials for this locomotive which, apparently, never mastered this part of the run within the required timings. The leading coach may here be carrying a transitional GWR/BR livery as it does not appear to have the GWR crest or 'GREAT WESTERN' legend. Compare this to the next two coaches which seem to have the GWR crest centrally below the waist. *19th May 1948*

For his photograph above, Norman was back at the lineside just to the south of Beam Bridge. The row of cottages seen in the distance by the Up side of the line has long since been demolished. The dwellings had been built by the railway company just a few years after this rural location temporarily became the 'end of the line' for twelve months during 1843-44, whilst the tunnel at Whiteball was completed.

Ex-LM&SR Motive Power on Trial

Black liveried Stanier Class '7P' 4-6-2 No. 46236 *City of Bradford* features again, this time whilst making the first of the outbound (Down) actual test runs. The former GWR dynamometer car is attached immediately behind the tender. Those responsible for such matters at Old Oak Carriage Sidings seemed to have been determined to show the GWR flag by assembling a train of modern, clean, large-window coaches and whilst they are not a 'matching set', they look very smart. The two behind the dynamometer car may be new Hawksworth designs. Again, this is on the climb towards Whiteball Tunnel, with the 1.30pm Paddington to Penzance. Norman recorded the time as 4.46pm; about 2 minutes down on the scheduled time between Taunton and Exeter, which C.J. Allen (ref. *The Locomotive Exchanges*, Ian Allan) noted as '*one of the most exacting of all point-to-point bookings*'. *18th May 1948*

Despite all the excitement brought about by the 'locomotive exchanges', the normal day-to-day traffic continued unaffected. Here, the 1.30pm Paddington to Penzance was worked by Laira based 'Castle' No. 5060 *Earl of Berkeley* (originally *Sarum Castle* until renamed in October 1937). The train was noted by Norman as 'right time' – perhaps the crew were determined to show what a 'Castle' could do? Compared to the train hauled by *City of Bradford* as seen on the previous page, on this occasion the two Hawksworth coaches towards the front are absent, some older coaches are present and the fourth may be a 'Dreadnought'. *5th May 1948*

Having photographed the visiting motive power working the pre-test train on this service during the Wednesday of the previous week (see page 140), perhaps Norman had returned to the lineside south of Beam Bridge seven days later expecting to see another of the 'exchange' workings. If so, No. 5003 may have come as somewhat of a disappointment to him, as this proved to be the only Wednesday within a period of several weeks when a pre-trial Down working was not booked to run!

DOUBLE-HOME WORKINGS

At 5.00pm exactly and with the shadows starting to lengthen on a lovely early May afternoon, Shrewsbury-based 'Castle' No. 5073 *Blenheim* (originally named *Cranbrook Castle*) storms up the bank with the 9.10am Manchester to Plymouth express. Note the immaculate external condition of No. 5073, so long a tradition of 'Salop' based locomotives. The leading five coaches seem to be ex-LM&SR, whilst those towards the rear of the train appear to be of GWR origin. Look at that delightful sky, by the way, again showing the benefits of scanning direct from the glass plate. *5th May 1948*

A 'Spam' at Temple Meads

'West Country' Class 4-6-2 No. 34006 *Bude*, carrying its new BR number but still otherwise immaculate in Southern Railway Malachite Green livery, attracts a small band of onlookers. Thankfully, in this view, the tender paired with the Bulleid 'Light Pacific' cannot be seen. The SR had no water-troughs and therefore no need to fit any pick-up apparatus to its locomotive tenders, so when working over 'foreign' lines during the 1948 'exchanges', standard ex-LM&SR tenders were used and these retained their plain black livery.

Norman recorded the date as 21st July 1948, which means he photographed the locomotive at Bristol immediately following the conclusion of the official trial run from Exeter. Completed in a set time of more than 12 minutes under the scheduled time, C.J. Allen described the run as 'one of the most outstanding of the entire test records over Western Region metals'; it included 35.8 miles knocked off at an average speed of 70.5 mph!

ABOVE: Despite the front buffers being obscured by the water column at the end of the station platform, we just had to include this one! When photographed here, No. 7007 – only recently allocated to Old Oak – was little more than two years old since placed new into traffic, in July 1946, as *Ogmore Castle*. This proved to be the last of the class completed before the demise of the GWR and so, at a ceremony at Swindon Works in January 1948, the locomotive was renamed *Great Western*. The coat of arms was added to the central wheel splasher on both sides of the locomotive. It is rather an irony, perhaps, that it is this locomotive, with its famous name, which is our first sighting within these pages of ex-GWR motive power coupled to a tender bearing the 'British Railways' legend! *22nd September 1948*
Apart from periodic visits to Swindon Works, No. 7007 became a long-term allocation to Worcester shed throughout the 1950s and until withdrawn (from Worcester) on 16th February 1963. The Ogmore Castle *nameplates were re-used, when No. 7035 – one of the final quartet of the Class to be built – was completed at Swindon in August 1950.*

BRISTOL TEMPLE MEADS

RIGHT: I imagine Norman took this shot of Swindon-based No. 5068 *Beverston Castle*, coming off shed at Bath Road, because it was paired with the experimental rigid 8-wheeled tender built in 1931. Other than the tender provided for the GWR Pacific *The Great Bear*, this was the only 8-wheeled tender built by the GWR. No. 5068 proved to be the eighth of eleven locomotives (twelve if you accept at least one reference) to which, in turn, the tender (No. 2586) is reported to have been attached. *6th June 1949*
No. 5068 acquired this tender during April 1949. The pairing lasted only five months, presumably until No. 5068 was called into Swindon Works in early November 1949 for a 'heavy general' repair. The May 1950 issue of the Railway Observer *reported the 'eight-wheeler' (in lined green livery) now attached to 'Star' Class No. 4043* **Prince Henry.**

Completed at Swindon in June 1948 and allocated to Bath Road, No. 7011 *Banbury Castle* was the fourth of the class to be released into traffic following Nationalisation. The interest here would have been the light green livery (not perpetuated by BR), the flush sided tender bearing the early style of full 'British Railways' legend, and the addition of a smokebox numberplate, No. 7011 having initially sported the number on the front buffer beam in traditional GWR style but here painted out. Not so obvious (but nonetheless soon spotted and reported in the *Railway Observer*), the omission of the speedometer drive more normally attached to the right-hand rear coupled wheel (the 'speedo', apparently awaiting the necessary parts, was fitted later). O.S. Nock described the lining out of the new livery as '*LNWR style*' and the overall effect he considered to be '*positively bilious*'! *22nd September 1948*

NORTH & EAST OF BRISTOL

'Castle' Class No. 5079 *Lysander* heads north with the 10.40am Penzance to Wolverhampton train, which also conveyed through carriages from Paignton and Torquay. Due off Bristol Temple Meads at 4.45pm, Norman recorded the time here as 5.10pm. He described this location only as *'near Yate'* and my guess is north of the town near Engine Common, on the stretch of line towards Rangeworthy and Wickwar Tunnel. The leading four coaches of this train will have come from Paignton, the remainder from Penzance. *31st August 1948*

Unusually, Norman Lockett used film negative for this photograph. David recalls clearly there was a major problem for his father in sourcing his usual glass plates for some months. It is clear that Norman struggled slightly with the new medium, which apparently involved the fitting of an adaptor to his camera (as detailed in the S&D volume) and it is noticeable that, as a result, he failed to allow enough foreground in the pictures taken on film stock. Lysander (originally named Lydford Castle) had been one of the five 'Castles' (No's 5039/79/83/91 and the converted 'Star' No. 100 A1 Lloyds) modified to oil burning but here only recently converted back to burn coal.

'Prairie' No. 5554 (allocated to Westbury shed) passes Foxes Wood, between St. Annes Park and Keynsham, with the 12.23pm Bristol-Bath stopping service. *3rd October 1949*

The large lineside tank and the water troughs were installed here in 1895, when all express traffic ran this way between London and the West Country or, via the Severn Tunnel, to South Wales. Later, after the construction of the direct (Westbury) route to Taunton and the Badminton direct line to South Wales, these troughs were much less used and, by the latter years of steam, only through trains between Brighton, Portsmouth and South Wales made regular use of the facility. The troughs were finally taken out of use in May 1961, after which locomotives took on water at the platform at Bath Spa.

NEAR COGLOAD JUNCTION

A new location visited by Norman in 1949, this is near Cogload Junction, where the routes from Bristol and Westbury come together north of Taunton. On an overcast early-afternoon, Norman positioned himself just to the side of the overbridge leading to Cogload Farm, east of the junction. This appears to be the only picture he took from this bridge; perhaps he found the location a little uninspiring. No. 5014 *Goodrich Castle* (allocated to Old Oak) is seen accelerating an express bound for Paddington across the Somerset Levels towards Athelney and Langport. *6th October 1948*
I think, judging from the appearance of the stock and the time recorded by Norman, this is the Up 'Torbay Express', of which the last four coaches had formed the 7.00am from Penzance and added to the 'Torbay' during a 10 minute stop at Newton Abbot. In this view, the Bristol route can be seen emerging in the distance on to the embankment leading to the flyover at Cogload, which lies just out of camera beyond the left margin.

A week later, Norman returned to Cogload, where to begin with he took this photograph of the Up 'Torbay Express', hauled by Newton Abbot based 'Castle' Class No. 5079 *Lysander*, which we saw just a few pages back, near Yate. The train appears to be comprised mostly of modern large window stock. *13th October 1949*
The Bristol route – part of the original 'Great Way Round' – passed through a cutting on the far boundary of the field on the right side of this view; the top of a signal post can just be made out. The flyover at Cogload (constructed in 1931) is used to carry the Down line of the Bristol route across both lines of the Westbury route, which had been completed by the GWR in 1906.

Just five minutes later, looking eastwards on the direct route via Westbury, 'King' Class 4-6-0 No. 6029 *King Edward VIII* draws near to Cogload with the 11.00am Paddington-Penzance, the corresponding Down working of the 'Torbay Express'. On an autumn day of bright sunshine, Norman recorded the train as running to time at 1.35pm. *13th October 1949*
The structure bridging the railway in the background housed, I believe, a water pipe. This was removed many years ago but the brick piers (or at least part of them) still exist.

EAST OF BURLESCOMBE

After several years of lineside visits (both pre- and post-war) to the Blackdown Hills on the eastern side of Whiteball Tunnel, in 1948 Norman crossed the Somerset/Devon county boundary to photograph scenes on the climb to the summit at Whiteball Siding Signal Box, on the western side of the tunnel. The gradients on this side are not as severe as those encountered on the westbound climb but, with just a few short breaks, extend for around 20 miles all the way from Exeter. The steepest gradient, 1 in 115, is over the final two miles towards the summit. This is the stretch of line which Norman elected to visit, between Burlescombe station and Whiteball box.

No. 2929 *Saint Stephen* and No. 4916 *Crumlin Hall* are highlighted by the bright Spring sunshine as they head for the summit of the eastbound climb to Whiteball, with what Norman described as the 7.40am Penzance-Bristol. John Lewis has pointed out, however, that he believes the 7.40am from Penzance was comprised of portions for Liverpool (GWR), Manchester (LM&SR), a Kingswear-Manchester coach (GWR) and Kingswear to Bristol (GWR) which included a dining car. That is very different to the formation seen here, so we will have to leave this one in the 'uncertain' category! *29th March 1948*
The assisting locomotive, No. 2929, dated from 1907 and would be withdrawn from Bath Road shed on 20th December 1949. No. 4916 was released into traffic in 1929 and lasted until withdrawn from Swindon shed on 8th August 1964.

THE HSBT PROJECT

As we near the end of this book, this seems an appropriate place to mention the HSBT Project. Anybody wishing to quote or source data regarding the withdrawal and scrapping of steam locomotives will be only too aware of just how frequently they have to resort to 'secondary sources' for such information. As a consequence (and here we quote from *The Railway Magazine,* November 2009) '*For more than twenty years, book authors and magazine writers have unwittingly perpetuated errors with regard to the withdrawal and scrapping of many BR steam locomotives.*' However, now a major project has been launched to set the record straight as to what really happened to steam. Known as 'The HSBT Project', this will research and publish the definitive record, as gathered only from primary sources, including official railway records and those of private sector scrapyards. This represents a major challenge and a time-consuming task. However, we are extremely pleased to be able to state that our own book is the very first that has benefited from the creation of The HSBT Project (still, in early 2010, very much in its infancy). Our thanks go to the Project and, in particular, to Roger Butcher (the member of the project with primary responsibility for Western Region data) who has, wherever possible, checked the post-1947 withdrawal and/or scrapping dates quoted by Mike in his captions. Pre-1948 data has not been checked by Roger, as this precedes the era to be covered by the Project. Finally, in case you are wondering, 'HSBT' is an acronym formed of the initial of the surname of each of the four people responsible for the Project!

This is a personal favourite. Norman was now looking eastwards towards the summit to photograph Mogul No. 6388 drifting slowly down the gradient with Class 'H' freight. The fireman gives a broad smile; was it for Norman's benefit or had he spotted the person (a signalman taking a 'short cut' to a turn of duty at Whiteball Siding box?) peddling his way uphill, between the Down main and relief lines! *29th August 1948*

ABOVE: A heavy loading of fourteen coaches for 'Castle' Class No. 5044 *Earl of Dunraven*. The first two coaches are of Hawksworth design, with domed ends and destination board brackets above the windows, instead of on the roof. (The roof boards seen here read 'Torbay Express', which is how Norman described the train.) Both these coaches appear to be in GWR livery. In contrast, the third coach is a 'Toplight' composite of 1906-21. The rearmost coaches may have been added en route; at Paignton perhaps? *29th August 1948*

If, as suggested, this was the 'Torbay Express', then the train must have been running out of schedule. The summer 1948 WTT shows a 10.20am (Sundays) Paignton-Paddington running via Castle Cary, having departed Exeter St. Davids at 11.54am. This, presumably was the 'Torbay Express', although it is not identified as such in the WTT. Norman's records state he photographed the train at 1.05pm!

Originally built as Beverston Castle in March 1936, No. 5044 was renamed in September 1937 and withdrawn in April 1962. The name Beverston Castle was reallocated to No. 5068 when that engine was released into service in 1938 and which, coincidentally, can be seen in the photograph on pages 146-7. No. 5044 remained an 'OOC' (later 81A) based locomotive from March 1936 (when new) until July 1960 and was withdrawn from Cardiff Canton on 3rd April 1962.

Having just passed the Up Distant signal for Whiteball, Salop-based 'Star' Class No. 4061 *Glastonbury Abbey* heads eastwards. Norman had this recorded as the 9.30am (Sundays) Plymouth to Paddington, which included through carriages from Kingswear and, like the 7.05am departure shown on the following page, ran via Bristol. However, as the train is composed entirely of ex-LM&SR stock, more likely it is the 10.00am (Sundays) Paignton to Bradford, here running just a few minutes behind schedule, which No. 4061 would work as far as Bristol Temple Meads. There, the train would be handed over to the LMR for the continuation of its journey northwards. *29th August 1948*

Built in 1922, No. 4061 is seen still running with inside steam pipes. Elbow type outside steam pipes were fitted somewhat belatedly in July 1949, No. 4061 proving to be one of the last of the 'Stars' to survive in service. She was withdrawn in March 1957. The leading coach, which is lined and is complete with LM&SR crest, appears to be a Stanier Period III design brake composite. Judging by its condition, this vehicle must have been repainted not too long before Nationalisation.

Prominent in the right background is the very large Westleigh Quarry. This was linked to the GWR at Burlescombe station, initially by means of a 3 foot gauge tramway nearly a mile in length. The tramway was replaced, in 1899, by a standard gauge private line. For many years, the quarry company dispatched the bulk of its stone and lime production by rail, in addition to supplying large quantities of track ballast to the GWR.

The driver of No. 4075 *Cardiff Castle* keeps a good lookout in charge of the 7.05am (Sundays) Plymouth to Paddington, a none too exacting service which called at many intermediate stations as far as Bristol (reached at 12.12pm), then continued – calling at main stations only – to reach Paddington at 3.50pm. *29th August 1948*

Had Norman made a print of this photograph, I suspect he might have adopted his more usual style and omitted at least some of the surrounds captured through the lens of his camera. However, by returning to the original glass plate negatives to scan the photographs for this book, we hope we have provided 'the best of both worlds', with some photographs as Norman might have presented them and many others, such as this example, illustrating the wider vista often to be discovered on his negatives.

A RETURN TO SOUTH DEVON

In August 1949, Norman made what appears to be a first visit back to the South Devon coast, the nearest he had reached to some of his pre-war lineside locations, a little farther to the west. About to pass on to the sea wall section at Langstone Rock, Newport (Ebbw Junction) based 'Mogul' No. 5364 passes Dawlish Warren and heads towards Dawlish with a Class 'D' freight bound for Hackney Yard, Newton Abbot. *21st August 1949*

This locomotive had been another of the class modified by increasing the weight to the front end (as described earlier in this book). As such, its number was changed to 8364 but when put back to original condition, as seen here, the engine reverted to its former number, 5364. Built in 1919, the locomotive was withdrawn 'from Newport) on 16th July 1951.

THE SEA WALL

With a Sunday occupation of the 'Down' line for engineering works, No. 5976 *Ashwicke Hall* runs 'wrong line' between Dawlish and Teignmouth with an excursion train. Judging from the stock, this appears to have originated from the Southern Region ('Ironclads', with a pair of Maunsell coaches in the middle), in which case No. 5976 more than likely took over when the direction of the train was reversed at Exeter St. David's. Having emerged from Parson's Tunnel, the excursion runs along the section of the sea wall towards Sprey Point. Parson's Tunnel Signal Box (the roof of which can just be seen over the first carriage) was 'switched out', hence the Up Home (also just visible) is pulled off despite the passage of this train in the opposite direction! *21st August 1949*

No. 5976, released new from Swindon in September 1938, was one of eleven 'Halls' converted temporarily to run as oil-burners for a period from 1946. This locomotive was converted in April 1947 and renumbered 3951 but reverted to coal burning and regained its original number in November 1948, the decision having been made by the government to abandon the costly scheme.

No. 6013 *King Henry VIII* emerges from Parson's Tunnel into bright sunlight with the Down 'Cornish Riviera', the stock of which appears to be in the new BR crimson & cream livery. Rather surprisingly, these are Collett large window stock rather than the most recent Hawksworth designs. The external cleanliness of No. 6013 (based at Old Oak Common) was yet to match pre-war standards. Economic times were still very hard and cleaners at a premium. Perhaps, however, a soiled coat in GW green was to be preferred to the blue livery which, the new Railway Executive had determined, was to be used to guild the 'Kings'. Thankfully, this edict persisted for only a short period of time and consequently not all of the class were destined to receive such treatment! *21st August 1949*

During the final decade of steam in everyday use over the former 'Great Western', Norman was destined to travel far more widely than previously, not least thanks to a chance meeting with fellow photographer Ivo Peters, which soon developed into a lasting friendship. However, as will become evident in the next volume of The Norman Lockett Archive, the area around Teignmouth (including, of course, 'the famous sea wall section) would become a favourite with Norman during the 1950s. In 1965, David Lockett moved to live, study and work in Teignmouth, which (as a favourite holiday location of this writer for very many years) is where I first met him and his wife, Daphne, in July 1988. This, in turn, led to a continuing friendship and collaboration to publish volumes featuring his father's photographs. So, taken all round, this is a very appropriate location at which to bring this book (almost!) to a close.

SUNSET OVER THE GREAT WESTERN

As daylight faded across the Great Western, Norman Lockett concluded yet another happy visit to the lineside. Just about to set off homewards, his attention was caught by a distant plume of steam. You must remember that inevitable reaction – time to stay put for 'just one more'! A Class '90XX' 4-4-0 heads a freight southwards – at no great pace – across the Somerset Levels.